The Madrona Project

Keep a Green Bough:
Voices from the Heart of Cascadia

THE MADRONA PROJECT
KEEP A GREEN BOUGH: VOICES FROM THE HEART OF CASCADIA

Empty Bowl, founded in 1976 as a cooperative letterpress publisher, has produced periodicals, broadsides, literary anthologies, collections of poetry, and books of Chinese translations. Our mission is to publish work by writers who share Empty Bowl's founding purpose, "literature and responsibility," and its fundamental theme, the love and preservation of human communities in wild places.

ISBN 978-1-7341873-8-0

Empty Bowl
14172 Madrona Drive
Anacortes, WA 98223
www.emptybowl.org
emptybowl1976@gmail.com

Printed at Gray Dog Press, Spokane, WA

Cover: Linda Okazaki, *Valley of Love in Birdland*
Back cover: Anita Leigh Holladay, *Luminance*
Illustrations on pp. 6, 11, 23, 33, 53, 56, 64, 84, 98, 104, and 111 by Susan Leopold Freeman

The Madrona Project

Volume II   *June 2021*   *Number 1*

KEEP A GREEN BOUGH:

VOICES FROM THE
HEART OF CASCADIA

Edited by Holly J. Hughes

Empty Bowl

Anacortes, Washington

CONTENTS

for Judith Roche

(1941–2019)

UPRIVER, THE SKAGIT

Here swiftly,
amid broken boulders
house-sized and strewn
far below the high cascade
descending almost from heaven,
amid the swirl and rush of water
dashing down and filling
the scatter of river-gouged pools,
broken necklace of moonstones
frothing at my feet, terraced
between brimming
turbulence of tumbled stone
slung from who-knows-where-
Anchorage, the Arctic-
volcanic events of rocks
unstrung and exploding
in the abyss
before beginnings,
before we had names,
to hesitate only briefly
in this watershed,
a moment on tiptoe
of geological time,
before clattering on
and the water rushing
down down down.

from *All Fire All Water*, Black Heron Press, 2015

PREFACE

Perhaps it's old news that the word anthology breaks down from the Greek as *anthos* (flower) + *-logia* (collection). This is quite lovely on its own, but when taken from a Straits Salish point of view there is an additional layer of meaning, for in addition to being beautiful, the flowers we prize and cultivate are also useful. Function and elegance are at the heart of our cultural aesthetic, and in the Salish Sea bioregion, the most beautiful flowers are also sources of nourishment, medicine, and warmth.

In the dirt below their shining blue blossoms, camas bulbs hold a unique, protein-rich carbohydrate that can be roasted and enjoyed immediately or dried and ground down into flour to be added to soups throughout the rainy winter. The blossoms of wild sweet roses become rosehips, a delicious source of beta carotene, vitamin C and other antioxidants, while radiant fireweed is vivid as well as versatile. Fireweed shoots can be eaten, its leaves can be made into tea, roots into medicine, and the downy seeds used as a fire starter or woven together with goat wool to make blankets.

There are many other examples of beautiful and useful botanicals in our homelands, but my point in examining the multifaceted function of native flora is to draw a comparison to the literature presented in the following pages. The blooms collected in this anthology are of a type that are beautiful to the mind's eye, and below the surface are nourishing to the spirit. Some may act as bitter medicine; some may fill a peculiar emptiness in you that you didn't know was there until you found you were filled up by what you'd read.

As you read these stories and poems by regional writers, please acknowledge the Indigenous storytellers and stories of this region, and how their words too often go unheard among the din of voices who've come here to use this land and its riches as a palimpsest.

This is also a land acknowledgment. And what is the point of a land acknowledgment? Is it to convince the descendants of colonizers to give tribes our land back? (Wouldn't that be nice?) The purpose of a land acknowledgment is to bring to the forefront of your attention a truth that often goes untold. A history that is rarely mentioned. This land was not empty when the first whites arrived. This land, these rivers, the tidelands, and the waterways – for the original inhabitants, this land was a garden, cultivated and cared for, cherished and understood.

This land is still loved by the descendants of the people who were forced from their homes and confined to small reservations; denied access to their usual and accustomed fishing, hunting, and harvesting areas. Denied their inherent right and spiritual obligation to gather nourishment in accordance with the cycles and rhythms of the seasons, and in accordance with our spiritual laws that ensured the continued prosperity of our camas fields, berry crops, fish runs, fowl flocks, and game.

To help us tend this garden, the ancestors provided intricate instructions that were passed down from generation to generation through traditional legends and stories. These stories contain teachings on how to live a beautiful life – how to live in a village alongside other people, how to live alongside the animal people, how to honor the gifts of the forests and the waterways so that they would continue to give their abundance. These stories are technology. A land acknowledgment asks you to ask yourself how you can make room for these stories, and for their tellers, and for the wisdom of how to care for our garden.

Rena Priest, Washington State Poet Laureate 2021–2023

Land Acknowledgment

First, a deep bow of gratitude to Rena Priest, Washington State Poet Laureate and member of the Lummi nation, for her eloquent preface and for reminding us that we all live on land that is the traditional territory of Indigenous tribes, tribes who have long cared for and continue to steward the lands and waterways of the Cascadia bioregion.

We acknowledge that Empty Bowl, based in Anacortes, Washington, is located on the traditional territory of the Samish and Swinomish peoples. I'm personally grateful to have roots in two communities: my cabin in Indianola was built on the traditional land of the Suquamish (Suqʷabš) tribe, the People of Clear Salt Water. I also live in the Chimacum Valley in the traditional and contemporary territories of the S'Klallam (Nə xʷsλ'áy̓ə m) and the Chemakum (Čə́mə q̓ə m) people. I'm grateful for the ongoing stewardship of it by their descendants, as well as to other local Indigenous nations who met, traded, and gardened in this area, including the Snohomish, Coast Salish, and the Makah. More recently, I acknowledge with deep gratitude many local tribes' generosity in sharing vaccines with their communities during the pandemic.

Wanting to honor the many tribal nations in our bioregion, I invited contributors to include a land acknowledgment in their biographies. Often, however, it's not possible to name the land as the territory of one tribe since many tribes may have passed through seasonally, and many were forced from their traditional lands by the government. I ask readers to understand that the contributors' land acknowledgments are by necessity brief but are offered in a spirit of gratitude, respect, and a growing awareness that our regional history is infinitely more complex than can be easily summarized here in a sentence.

Most of all, I want to acknowledge that acknowledging the land is only a start. As the Honor Native Land website points out, "Acknowledgment by itself is a small gesture. It becomes meaningful when coupled with authentic relationship and informed action. But this beginning can be an opening to greater public consciousness of Native sovereignty and cultural rights, a step toward equitable relationship and reconciliation." In that spirit, I commit to the work of humble and respectful relationship, recognizing that the long history of broken trust will take time to heal and I have much to learn. As Rena Priest wisely suggests, we begin by "asking ourselves how to make room for these stories, and for their tellers, and for the wisdom of how to care for our garden."

Holly J. Hughes, editor

Honor Native Land website: https://usdac.us/nativeland
Native Land map: https://native-land.ca/

INTRODUCTION

Keep a green bough in your heart, the singing bird will come

Out my window, tall Douglas firs march down the hillside. Through them the Salish Sea shimmers in faint winter sun. Beyond lies Eastsound and the curve of Orcas Island, like a horseshoe where it narrows. Behind me stretch twenty-five acres, owned by the people who built the cabin I'm grateful to be staying in this week. I'm also deeply aware of the presence of the Coast Salish, who harvested clams and fished for salmon—and all who lived on and passed through these islands long before Europeans arrived.

On my desk is a copy of *Digging for Roots: Works by Women of the North Olympic Peninsula*, edited by Christina V. Pacosz and Susan Oliver and published by Empty Bowl in 1985. Inside are black-and-white photographs, artwork, poetry, and stories by women of the Olympic Peninsula, women who were raised here, women who chose to move here, and a few Indigenous women whose people were here for millennia. United in time and place, their writing reflects a sense of shared sisterhood: women making their way in what was clearly a male world, a time when forests were measured in board feet and trees were falling, the tag end of decades in the Northwest reaping the abundance of the land and sea to build an economy that we were just starting to realize could not be sustained.

Three decades later, there's clearly more digging to do to get to the root of what's brought us to this precarious place as a nation and a planet. This morning I'm wanting to get to the root of root. The etymological dictionary tells us this: Middle English *rote, root, roote*, "the underground part of a plant," Old Norse *rot*, from Proto-Germanic *wrots*, but the proto-Indo-European lists cognates with *radish* and *radix,* which share a root with *radical.* And like that, we've gone from root to radical, a leap that seems fitting in these times that call for rootedness and radical words. To share stories during dark times has long been a necessary, radical act.

In that spirit, I'm honored to serve as editor for volume 2 of *The Madrona Project,* a volume that we're choosing to again devote to women. For this issue, I invited not only women of the North Olympic Peninsula but women of the Cascadia bioregion—Alaska and Oregon as well as Washington—and to again include voices of Indigenous women, voices that have too long been silenced. During the profound uncertainty of 2020 I turned to writing to keep me afloat, and I suspect others did the same. So I invited others to share their reflections on what it means to be living and writing in Cascadia in these historic times. Here's what I wrote in the call for submissions, sent January 1, 2021:

> It's an understatement to say these are challenging times. I want to believe we're at a hinge moment, an inflection point, awaiting what will emerge from the unprecedented upheaval that marked 2020. While the pandemic is not yet behind us, we see a dim light on the horizon and our democracy, shaky though it may be, is still intact. We have been painfully reminded that we must rebuild a democracy that acknowledges systemic racism and that will provide justice for all its people. The rifts in our economic system are starkly evident, and I hope we're re-envisioning an economy that honors the diverse histories, lives and voices of all who shape it, as well as the land and

sea upon which it depends. Every day brings us undeniable evidence that climate change is here and we're living with its consequences; the years ahead will surely test our capacity for resilience.

But we live in the Cascadia/Salish Sea bioregion, shaped by wind, water, the traditions and wisdom of the Indigenous people who paddled these waters, and the stories of our ancestors who were drawn to the Northwest. We're surrounded by towering Douglas fir and cedar, where salmon still return each fall, eagle and osprey soar in our grey skies, and kingfishers and blue herons wait, patient, for a glint of fish. How does this inform our work as writers in this bioregion?

So, I'm asking you, my sister writers, to reflect on this moment in history and place and write about what challenges, engages, or sustains you as we head together into whatever's ahead in 2021.

This issue is the result of their responses; I invite you to dig in. Here's a brief taste of what you'll find:

These writers remind us that our lives in Cascadia are still interwoven with fir and cedar, salmon and kingfisher, heron and eagle, raven and crow—and perhaps even more so as we face an uncertain future together. Climate change is no longer off in the distance; it is here, as devastating forest fires in Oregon and Washington the last two summers made painfully visible. Meanwhile, less visibly, the oceans are warming, sending ripples out through the food chain as Chinook salmon runs continue to decline, threatening our resident orca populations. Yet, as many of the writers remind us, we still look to the natural world for signs of resiliency and hope, acknowledging all the ways the natural world has sustained us during the pandemic.

These pieces span generations: women writing about their mothers, great-aunts, and grandmothers; women reflecting on coming of age and aging together. In *Digging for Roots* from 1985, Port Angeles poet Alice Derry's poem describes an intimate moment with her husband. Three decades later, in Derry's poem for this collection, she grieves his passing. Kate Reavey reflects on the generations in her family as she makes blackberry jam. And after growing up in a small town on the Kitsap Peninsula, Irene Keliher reflects on the native blackberry and what it means to be native to a place as she raises her two sons in urban Seattle.

These pieces span geography: women write about their personal connections with the land and sea from Prince William Sound, Alaska, to Cape Flattery, Washington; from the Spokane and Duwamish Rivers to the green valleys of Oregon. Tess Gallagher reflects on her two Northwests: growing up in Port Angeles and time spent at her cottage in Western Ireland; Alaska writer Carolyn Servid asks what we might learn from the stories of the Indigenous peoples; Claudia Castro Luna reflects on what it means to love a place as she drives across eastern Washington bringing poetry to underserved areas as Washington State's poet laureate.

These pieces speak up, acknowledging the painful history of the Indigenous nations who've weathered the suppression of their culture. Here, you'll find Sandra Jane Polzin's map of her grandmother's voyage from her village on the Nass River down to Seattle in

1923. You'll find K'Ehleyr McNulty's poem "Unprecedented," reminding us that this isn't the first pandemic. You'll read Sara Marie Ortiz's braided essay "River," which ends with a description of her moving letter to the next generation, a theme echoed in Kristen Millares Young's searing questions to future readers: "Shall we tell them that ours was among the first generations to listen to women, and that when we spoke it was a howl? That the earth spoke and we did not listen?"

Throughout this collection, writers bear witness to the hard truths not only of our history but of current inequities laid bare by the pandemic and the consequences of centuries of exploitation of the earth. They invite us to consider the existential question of our time: how might we envision a future that's sustainable and just, a future that honors the earth and all her peoples as well as all her kin—the word that botanist and citizen of the Potawatomi Nation Robin Wall Kimmerer suggests we use to refer to our more-than-human neighbors.

The powerful image on the cover by artist Linda Okazaki is taken from *The Conference of the Birds* by Farid Ud-Din Attar, written in 1177, and illustrates the second chapter, "The Valley of Love." It opens when all the birds of the world gather to begin their search for an ideal king. After a long journey, led by the hoopoe, they arrive to find that the leader they sought is, of course, themselves.

In 2021, as together we resume our journey toward a just and sustainable future, there are glimmers of hope. Skunk cabbage raised her yellow lanterns from the ditches after a long, dark winter; cherry trees burst into outrageous, fragrant blossom. We have new leadership in Washington DC setting long overdue, ambitious carbon-reduction goals and filling cabinet level positions with people who finally represent our diverse nation, including our first Indigenous cabinet member, Secretary of the Interior Debra Haaland. New scientific research is emerging to support what the Indigenous peoples have long known: the trees are talking to each other and have wisdom to share. Perhaps this will be the year that, as Tele Aadsen writes in her essay "Change," "we do the unexpected, do the hard thing, when we go off-script and show what we truly value. When the storm continues but we're not passive. When we reach for the tools before us—science, history, culture, art, community, love—and we make a change."

The title of this collection comes from an ancient Chinese saying: "Keep a green bough in your heart, the singing bird will come," words that resonate on many levels. And as former Oregon Poet Laureate Kim Stafford reminds us, "We have not arrived to explain but to sing. . . Songbird guards his twig, his only weapon his song." I hope our songs will spark your imagination, rekindle, and breathe life into these embers of hope. Together, may we envision a future that hears and honors all our voices.

Holly J. Hughes
May 2021

JOCELYN CURRY
LA PUSH

To observe and sketch the natural world around us can take us to a place of wonder and awe. Jocelyn Curry, at the age of twelve, began journaling with added sketches and has never stopped. Later, her study of calligraphy enhanced her ability to see line quality in nature. Teaching calligraphy and nature journaling required her to formulate lessons to reliably help students learn to see not only letter forms, but forms and colors in nature. Practicing drawing quickly and allowing spontaneity serve us well when we may be uncomfortable drawing outdoors, or when our subject is changing before our eyes! Jocelyn lives in Shoreline, WA, with her husband of forty-six years, many sentinel red cedars and Douglas firs, and one twelve-year-old hen, named Cinnamon.

MARYBETH HOLLEMAN
WET

West Twin Bay

In a rainforest, it rains. But the rain doesn't just fall to the ground, soak into soil. It covers everything. It clings so completely that even after the rain stops falling from the sky, even when the sun has shone all day, it still rains. On me. As I walk through it. The trail is spongy with sphagnum moss, and my feet get wet. Even the driftwood planks laid across the muddiest spots are wet, and I slip on mossy wood. Skunk cabbage, as big as my three-year-old son and studded with diamonds of rain, slaps my legs, spraying water. Slender grasses, green orchid, purple aster, and ladies' tresses shiver as I pass, releasing more liquid. This rain is like seeds that disperse by attaching to a passing animal's fur, so easily do I gather rain to my body. Droplets seem to jump out onto me, as if dry is simply an abstract concept here, as if an equilibrium of wet on all things must be maintained. Onward. I scramble up a hill, grabbing onto roots. Now salmonberry and blueberry wave wet against my hips. Spruce and hemlock saplings rub my shoulders and pat my back with wet needles. A passing breeze coats my hair and face in the lifeblood of this forest. If I stay here long enough, will the hair on my arms grow moss? Will tendrils of old-man's-beard hang around my face? Will my feet sink even deeper into black soil until I am rooted in place?

MARYBETH HOLLEMAN
BEAR

Picturesque Cove

Low tide, and the shallow cove is nearly drained. We haul the boats high on the beach, dragging their hulls across a field of dead and dying salmon. The acrid stench of decay fills the air as persistently as a cloud of mosquitoes on caribou. Their bodies, some crippled by death into grotesque forms, have faded from brilliant red into the same mottled gray as the mud that now holds them. A swarm of glaucous and herring gulls hop and flap, pecking at the worn-out bodies, snatching eyeballs from those still living, leaving them blind in their last moments.

Above the beach ryegrass, I walk the trail to the cabin. Beside it, the stream is clogged with fins like daggers carving water. At the sound of a splash, I turn. A few feet away stands a black bear, salmon in mouth. It lifts a shaggy head toward me, the small round ears twitching, then it gallops, bowlegged, out of the stream and up the near-vertical bank into the woods.

I run to the cabin and latch the wooden door.

Later, I step out on the porch to hang wet clothes. A black bear in the stream, another on the bank, both freeze. I freeze, too. They stand no taller than I, but are thick with fur and muscle. If one were to lunge forward toward the deck, it would have me.

The bear in the stream breaks the trance: it swipes at the water with a wide paw, catches a writhing fish, dashes up the bank. The other enters the roiling water, high-stepping to avoid slipping on salmon.

Far into the late-summer evening, the bears fish the stream right beside the cabin. They must know I'm not a hunter. They must know that bear-hunting season arrives after the salmon are gone, when they fill their bellies with salmonberry and blueberry instead of fish, when they begin dreaming of long winter nights in dark dens.

These two excerpts from my memoir, The Heart of the Sound, *appear in the book as short prose pieces between longer narrative chapters. The story takes place in the marine wilderness of Prince William Sound, Alaska. These excerpts are moments of being so present in the place that the veil drops, allowing for connection and insight into the lives of the more-than-human world.*

RONDA PISZK BROATCH
SHOOTING THE BEAR – HIGH DIVIDE TRAIL

I pick my way through root and granite,
to pack stashed beneath fallen old-growth
cedar. Hermit thrush, her

A —

F —

E —

flat notes float from the understory.
Across the Sol Duc, passing Lover's Lane Trail
I tumble the words:

switchback, bear scat, prized
purple *Vaccinium membranaceum* on my tongue.
Breathe, and repeat

advice a hiker once gave me:
when the bear came to me, I put aside the hungry beast
of my camera.

Ursus americanus, your small eyes,
keen nose now measure our distance. I quiet
the clack of trekking pole

against stone, hide
behind my lens, rush of inhale, exhale, sing to
this season for lingering

in avalanche
lily, your full-moon gaze
reflecting mine.

ANNA LINZER
FIRST LIGHT

In the cove below the Treehouse

there is a single spotted harbor seal.

The only one in the bay,

maybe in the world this morning.

She slips beneath the water and flies

just under the still surface.

Diving deeper, she takes with her

the rest of my day,

leaving only her slender brushstroke of white

light in the pewter grey dawn.

GREEN

outside under the warmed rainwater, showering, I stare into the green of the spruces and hemlocks and cedars beyond the small clearing in this patch of rain forest that still lives, still grows, still breaths, still drips with lichen and moss and fern along this river and I find myself again dizzy with all the shades of winter's green being invaded by spring's thrust of bud and leaf and branch. a box for a crayola 120 pack of crayons would not have room for all these shades of moss and needle and leaf and grass and lichen and vine, each holding its own array of green, not just species, but each tree, each plant. each side – north east south west – holding its own color chart. I want to say, look, look at the greens, but I am alone in a downpour of cold march rain and warm rainwater in the quiet clearing. and spring is just one season, today is just one day. this is just one place in just one forest. tomorrow the light will shift. the yellows and greys and browns and whites and reds and more will always have their way with these greens. I know the shower is running long, pulling rainwater from the corrugated metal tank, standing modestly grandly shyly boldly alone under cedar and vine maple, attached to the gutters by a single pipe like an umbilical cord to the heavens. but a day of hard rain gives me more water, more time to soak these greens into eye and skin and heart. drunk on greens with no name, I turn the shower off and reach for my green towel, knowing it is not even a near relative to the green feast beyond me, knowing it holds *green* like a stolen title.

and for this one green moment, the virus is gone. just like that. my aching heart is filled with a warmth like clear rainwater on my skin, washing out the dis-ease of sorrow and fear.

SKYE LEVARI
I WAS BORN FROM THE RAIN

Looking out the same window, bitter
       coffee easing the knots in the temples.
              Clouds skate the sky, a cold blue steady

beneath the wind's mouth. Truthfully,
       it is the same graceful cedar gown,
              boughs easy under gravity, skin wet leather

under a pruned palm. Or the maple,
       now all bony elbows & knuckles, moss
              shivering upward. Or even the blackberry,

dying in November, again, before
       angry & beautiful next year. Or the child,
              who refuses to wear his rain jacket, telling me

I was born from the rain,
       which I would never dispute
              & the same soaking day is a sponge

expanding, swelling, with diligent attention.

MARYNA AJAJA
CHIMACUM COWS

They arch their perfect backbones

                in the sun

                        on the hillside,

      though massive clouds

                   cross about

they face due east

      in perfect need of random,

                  while the possibility of rain

     is sacred

                  in some languages.

PORT TOWNSEND

I walk to the store and buy a postcard of Venice.

The watery view of Port Townsend is clear.

The wind is crazy as a prairie woman.

Monet's gondola is out of line with the quay.

Everything here is lavender.

The ferry sidles in from Whidbey Island

its furious rudder plows foam.

I walk the one hundred thirty-eight steps past Galatea.

There are no people in the postcard.

Nothing keeps the viewer from the water.

Venice is a long way off.

SAMANTHA DELLA DEVONEY
CAPE FLATTERY

Standing at the beginning

The edge with a panoramic view

100-foot drop to the churning gut

Of the opening to the vast Pacific Ocean

Surging through the glacier cut

Chasm, cupping the salty water

Moving easily east to the Salish Sea

The gateway, Standing at the hinge

Ancestral look out

Directly ahead, Standing erect and proud

The only sign of colonization, a lighthouse

In this rural, wild site

On Tatoosh Island: Traditional fishing, sealing, whaling camp, and hiding place

Myriad of greens standing like

Ancestors having your back

Water: 180 degrees; forested cliffs: 180 degrees

Vancouver Island across the mouth in the distance

100% Teaming with life sounds

Oystercatchers squawking, running in and out

Ebb and flow fully realized

On this cliff.

Wind blowing strongly

Scent of the vast oceans, Reminding of the Fluid Power

A vortex of Energy

Sea lions barking letting us know they are here

As we are.

MEREDITH PARKER
TO BEAR WITNESS

Waning autumn sun shrouded.
Exposed skin feels remnants of the day's warmth.
Bare feet tell of walking straight, then sharply right to examine a shell,
then wandering left to the shimmer of jelly fish cast ashore to dry
by the last wave of the receding tide.

Inanimate objects in the sand, still, noticeable.
The waves pull in, curl and lap
as the moon rises over the trees
and the oranges and reds dominate the evening sky.
Click of crab feet scurry in business-like manner

And then there he is:
plumage of dark black, stark white and a distinctly orange bill,
eyes green as the changing tides at Tatoosh.
Particles of sand dot the feathers of the wing
as he lay to one side looking up, his eye to mine.

How many miles of ocean waves, storms, star-filled nights,
the spouting of whales as they head north, then south, with purpose?
The freighters that spew, the fishers that cast their nets.
How many chicks were born, how has his history passed
within the DNA of his own folk?

Eyes locked, I slowly sit beside his once proud form,
wanting to lay a gentle hand to his back,
but resist and instead mimic his breath:
In, out, chest rising and falling,
I'm suddenly overcome with grief.

Here at this moment to bear witness,
to acknowledge the life that was, the immensity of his travels,
the sweetness of flight, wings tirelessly pumping,
ache of hunger right before a small fish is swallowed,
sating, fulfilling, free, and then it is time.

For he knew when he descended to the top of the water,
carried with the currents, surrendering,
that it was the end. And it was I who saw the last blink,
heard the final shudder of his breath.
And felt the strange pang of love in that moment of death.

SIERRA GOLDEN
SOME GHOSTS

Many residents of the Pacific Northwest are aware of stories alleging that a specific run of particularly large chinook salmon, the so-called "June hogs," once migrated up the Columbia River. . . . We found no empirical evidence indicating that a unique population of massive fish ever existed in the Columbia River.

~ National Oceanic and Atmospheric Administration Technical
Memorandum NMFS-NWFSC-22, July 1995

A lady wears pearls, my mother said,
A lady wears pearls and slippers and skirts.
I'd rather wear these lures. I found them

in God's pocket. I feel beautiful
with one dangled from my ear. Cheap metal
hammered into a dimpled silver flasher.

The green bead matches my eyes.
The barbed treble hook is cold
on the tender skin below my jaw.

I think the lure is just as good or better
than pearls. Plus, I could lift it
from my ear and catch a June hog

on the river. I dream of hooks
and boots and pants. In real life,
I caught a salmon on the Columbia,

at sundown the water like a copper plate
and the fish big as a hay bale and heavier,
hard even for the biggest farm boy to lift.

Yes, I landed it myself,
saying a little prayer under my breath
but not what you think.

I prayed for the fish's strength. I prayed
not for the win but the fight. I felt
the rapture of being alive and gave thanks.

I praised God and her pockets
where I might find something
both useful and beautiful as a hook.

I took the stilled fish to be sold and kept
my mother alive with the supplies I bought.
She told me, *A lady doesn't fish.*

Now the June hogs are gone, dammed
out of existence, and scientists say there is
no empirical evidence they ever existed.

No one ever asks me, and so
what I don't say is that some ghosts are real.
I touched their muscled flanks with bare hands.

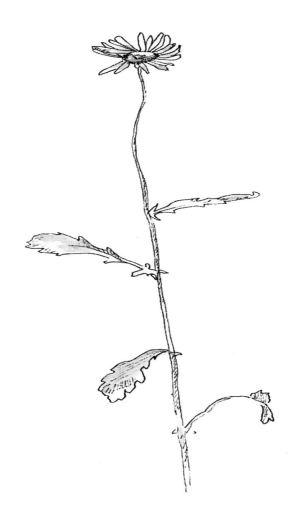

CARMEN GERMAIN
BUTTERBUR (AND WILD PANSY)

on a painting by Morris Graves

Pure luminosity, the butterbur, scarlet off-white frothing, striking and spirited,
each stamen's pinpoint of light

in a skyrocket of smoke and noise, the way happiness
like a festival takes over, fireworks staving off darkness

in a barrage of pyrotechnics.

In a translucent bottle, purple-blue petals in five directions, a wild pansy
poses next to this ballistic. It's said violets grew wherever
Orpheus put down his lyre

and I like to think because he honored music so much —

his beautiful song — the viola spreads its leaves
to open more to listening.

Three red-orange rosehips

lean forward, alert to the darker tone of these petals,
how men prefer this shade while women, like Persephone,
are drawn to the lighter. Still the butterbur catches our eye first,

stolid in its bronze vessel. How it thrusts shoulders forward
like someone in charge about to shout orders.

But it's the wild pansy where I keep returning, how it emerges
from milky glass *not* shrinking, how two leaves rise like hands

to praise the fragile peace.

GEORGIA JOHNSON
THE COLOR OF AIR

Even after years of attention
to standard avian detail,
beak made for seeds and nuts
or beak made for prying insects,
the ping-ping-zee of a young junco
in October
or the alphabet-defying lilt and trilled
twirling pair of redwing blackbirds
in May,
I am surprised and suspect of the name
chosen for red-breasted nuthatch.
For so many years of Julys
I could not see or hear it,
fixated on a small svelte back
dusted with opal mirage blue, hints of
eye-shadow blue, wash of blue sky with
cloud skeins passing through.
Searching my Merlin app for blue
reflected by lake on a one-hundred-degree day,
smaller than a robin, no, not a chickadee.
Agile and upside down on feeder or cedar bark –
I could not name it until today.
Someone thought that common red breast more
particular than the color of air at ten thousand
feet brought down to me on earth.

KATE REAVEY
AUGUST 2020

When is the door not a door?
When it is ajar.

I
A joke Tom used to tell returns
as I wash the lids for the jam

then boil them, and berries
sit in a colander, wait to be rinsed.

The door being ajar
is not danger, not today.

With summer fully present, a jar
becomes a kind of welcome,

an invitation to enter – and the door ajar
is a way a teen tells her mother

it is okay – maybe – to come in, but first,
please knock.

Even though the opening is here,
this entryway is also private.

II
And when the last jar
of last year's trailing blackberry jam is cracked open –

the batch that took four trips
on that small circle of trail on the DNR lands,

while we waited for more to ripen,
the summer before masks were required –

our grown son is asleep, upstairs, too far away
to notice the delight of this moment.

III
I am here, a mother, a woman
who was once that teen-aged daughter

with her door cracked open just enough
to let in a little bit of light.

This morning I am making coffee, allowing
the dark roast to mix with a swirl of cream,

telling myself old jokes, and just briefly
noticing the possibility

that my own mother might whisper
from the other side of everything.

I let our son sleep in – remember the berries –
a year ago, ten years ago, four decades ago,

as if I might taste the rain, the sun,
alongside the bitter seeds –

and dip my spoon into the open jar.

JEAN HALLINGSTAD
PANTOUM: AFTER THE BONFIRE COOLS

This garden has roots that mine our souls.
The spade turns up a cache of stone.
Blackberries stain the grass and soles of our feet
and mourning cloaks worry the dying oak.

The spade turns up its cache of stone
in island soil: not fit for farming.
Mourning cloaks worry the dying oak
and the air is luminous with dust.

Island soil: not fit for farming.
Anger spent, their broken dishes ended here
where the air is illumined by their dust.
We've turned our sorrows into clay.

Anger spent, their broken dishes ended here.
My grandmother drew circles to conjure up rain.
We've turned our sorrows into the clay
and by night the upstairs window dreams aloud.

My grandmother drew circles to conjure up rain.
We sleep these days with one ear awake
for what by night the upstairs window dreams.
We scatter ashes to sweeten the fruit

and sleep with one ear always awake.
Blackberries stain the grass and soles of our feet.
We scatter his ashes to sweeten the fruit.
This garden has roots that mine our souls.

SALLY GREEN
AUNT MABEL TALKS ABOUT BIRDS

It's the western meadowlark I think back on most,
a voice that shimmered like heat waves
over alfalfa and wheat fields, pasturelands
spread on all sides of the farm. That was the view
from our hayloft. Most out-of-staters felt off-kilter
under a sky stretched to fit the size
of Montana. Mother loved it, bragged
that when she saw a buggy jouncing
over farm-road ruts, she'd have fruit cobbler
hot from the oven and a fresh pot of coffee
all set on the table before visitors pulled up
by the front stoop and shouted out greetings.

Like most back then, our family was large. We each
had daily chores. I got bored with dishes,
laundry, and figuring out a share of meal-making
with bossy sisters. I wanted to join my brothers
getting in the hay, following the plow,
or shearing the sheep. My real talent seemed to be
getting in the way. I doubt anyone took notice
when I stomped off to the shady backside
of a storage shed. I'd sit there, stock-still,
hid among twists of barbed wire, rusted
bedsprings, battered washtubs. Barn swallows
nested in the eaves. With eyes squeezed tight
I listened to the clamor of chicks rise and fall
as parents swooped in with flies snatched
from sheep pens. Sometimes a bobolink's song, flashy
as its straw-colored cap, drifted in. When I heard
a meadowlark, I had to sit up, find the fencepost
it perched on, watch him tip his head skyward
and sing out for a lady friend. Those birds
didn't mind my being there, and I grew
to need the ease that came over me.

It was marriage took me away. We settled into
city jobs, raised our child. Birdsongs echoing
off buildings, or rising from ornamental trees
that lined the streets, weren't the same as home. Clamor
of business and traffic dulled their voices.
Thoughts of birds back on the farm always brought
up the sorrowfuls. Most of my seventy years
were spent in that city. After I buried my Elmer
I felt like a bird blown off course. Most everyone

17

I knew was gone – moved away or passed. When
my daughter wrote, "Mom, just come!" I did, west
to Washington, a log house on an island. At first
I felt squeezed in by all the trees taller than grain
silos, anxious for sky bigger than patches
on a hired man's britches. Felt like the world
had withered up. It was birds again that saved me,

first the winter wren, that sweet trill that lifted out
of tangled brush year-round. Then the black-headed
grosbeak. Putting a name to that jaunty string
of notes sung from behind a screen of maple leaves
was a challenge. Even a glimpse of it was thrilling
as the shiny medal I won in a sixth-grade spelling
bee. Crossbills brought to mind a chatty clutch
of friends in kitchens after church. Chickadees
were clowns in a circus ring. On walks to loosen
up my joints, resting in any rag of sun I could find
in the yard, we got acquainted. Songs, calls, even
the soft sounds of wingbeats come through a window
screen said names in my head, brought a calm
I hadn't known since girlhood. My daughter
likes to tease, says I'm the sort of fussbudget
can't pass a tilted picture on a hallway wall
without stopping to straighten it. And she's right,
but there's also the matter of being straightened,
set back to center. I hear a meadowlark in my head,
think of birds I'll likely not see again, recite the new
names, and feel a little nudge putting me straight,
balanced, looking out at a world that suddenly
makes more sense.

JANA HARRIS
THE FIRST TEN ACRES

Mary Robinson Gilkey, b. 1846, Oregon Country

At the end of her life,
Mother often recalled the early years:
The loamy bottomland cleared.
Twenty pokes of wheat seed borrowed,
every kernel accounted for, secreted
inside the oxcart where she
and her new husband slept
keeping it safe and warm.

Father, Grandfather, my uncles,
even the smallest brother slicing
into unbruised sod with
wooden mold-board plows.
To the west an immovable wave
of coastal hills, to the east
the river a darker blue than the sky
and beyond
a ridge of white saw teeth
that gave off light even in the clear darkness
of moonless nights.
My mother, grandmother, the aunts
carried water, the scent of fir rising,
a breeze gusting into chorus
trust us, trust us
like the answer to some call.

Mornings, after coffee
made from ground roasted peas
boiled over an open fire,
her bare hands, fingers clawed, grabbed
loose black clods the shape of hearts,
anchoring, covering, wetting,
each seed as she sang me rhymes
though I was as yet only a wish

— *and the green grass grows all around, all around*
and the green grain grows all around.

Sowed, harrowed in with the three oxen
and two cows that survived;
harvested by extemporized scythes,
shafts laid straight, heads up, shingle style

19

the grain threshed by the might
of sharp horse hooves trodden over it, then
the straw piled on bed sheets,
fanned, separated by hand:
forty bushels to an acre.

My mother, young, her face unlined
and filled with hope
as she inhaled the covenant, dropped
each seed into a black well of earth.
Married only a month,
her happiness never again
so simple or untroubled as she dreamed
the smell of ersatz coffee
made from their first parched wheat.
If she could have back
one bygone morning, Mother told me,
it would be end of May, 1845,
when the wheat first greens
like a shawl of changeable silk
and every bitter thing tastes sweet.

BARBIE BROOKING
JANUARY MORNING

In memory of Steve Kikuchi

Loon rests on the water,
dips her beak as if to sip the brine,
as if to peek into the world below.

Loon dives,
and the waters barely part –
as if Loon loves both worlds so completely
the barriers disappear.

Five times we've circled the sun without you.
Now, in the muted light of this January morning,
we reach to touch the ripples left
when you slipped out of sight.

ALICE DERRY
LOST AND FOUND

> *Then practice losing farther, losing faster*
>
> ~ Elizabeth Bishop

I lost sunset. I lost the stars, fog returning.
On darkening sand, I found a mottled eagle feather.
That will be for Theresa, her weaving.

I've lost all the nights to come, camping with you.
Without your shoulders, my narrow one-person tent
is all I can carry. Coffin tent, I call it,
to go with my mummy bag.

I don't know yet what I've found –
where the two big opposites, land and sea, edge together
among a scatter of drift logs, shells, and spongy seaweed carpets,
ruckus of birds and surf. Nothing changes
but each moment feels different.

I don't know yet if I've found what I can live with.
You aren't scuffing this sand beside me,
our first courtship hike together.
But I have no way to lose you in the echoes of the night years later
when we couldn't sleep for sea lions' barking.

I keep looking to agree with someone –
shall we hike now, shall we eat, nap in the tent?
If I step without you into the unknown, I might find it possible.

Sanderlings rise as one body, their strict formation aloft.
They are never alone, landing to stilt-run the tide line.
Unconcerned, a ragged stretch of oystercatchers inks the gray.

I am *one* here, speak to no one except any hiker's hello.

The second morning, I lost the promised sun, straggling out of my tent
into mist. Glad my stove worked.

What found me were four river otters, sleek in the waves. Once on sand,
their tails weighty, they tumbled forward,
then back. When I froze to driftwood, they could dash
to their creek-side den.

Wading the creek, I followed tide's sight line until rain came.

I missed you every moment – how much you hated camping in sand,
how many times you came anyway for the wild of it.

The wild rose up in me, as it does when I go into it, expecting nothing
and on the friendly beach make my frail home against a bank, under scaled spruce,
among sea-rocket. They aren't letting me or refusing me.

Losing doesn't allow itself to be pure and unatoned.
Finding, no compensation, pours like flood tide onto the beach.
We know the living and dead are entwined, but here, where I am never
without tide's losing and finding,
why should the twining be so finally unknowable?

Like Rilke's lovers, we lay here that first time, all the wildness loose in us, thinking
ourselves one,
thinking no further than one.

CHARLOTTE G. WARREN
A TIME TO LIVE AND A TIME TO DIE

My time now
is a time to die. Not at once, but soon.
I'm grateful for this house
warm and full of light,
our children's voices like handprints
covering the walls of my heart.

The ragged edges of getting along,
the sweet moments of closeness, all of us
pitching in to hoist a canoe to the top of the car,
remembering the paddles, the sandwiches, life jackets,

and how at last we hauled our craft over the hummocks of sand-grass
into the pebbly shallows, pant legs rolled up, one foot,
then another shaking the water off, getting inside,
pushing off, afloat. That holy silence. Seawater

sliding off the paddles, salt air and sun
opening the sky around us.

Or how, in the fall, the geese call us out, their wavering vee's.
How we lie on our backs in the dark, talking quietly,
waiting for the Perseid showers to scatter the sky.

This house, these loves, I must let them go. The moon's
lantern in the Douglas fir, the Cooper's hawk settled on the railing,
butterflies, rainbows.

Why was I so often sad in the midst of all this glory? As if
the world was broken and I couldn't mend it? As if I myself
would never mend, when mountains rise and fall, and the sea itself
unravels its shores. Love endures.

I give you mine. I hold yours.

KATHRYN HUNT
ASH-BOAT

1

Each Wednesday noon, the town
alerts us to disaster with five notes
from *Close Encounters.* They gentle us
toward our losses. What happens
in Japan reaches here, only higher.
Sun on waves, chill in November
ground. Each thing folded into
its other self.

Kathy's head is crowned in circling
elegance, paisley cloth woven in
Morocco lending her a way to marry
corresponding bewilderment of ease
and chemo into the telling of her day.
The waffles warm us through. We let
our talk raise a world whole enough
to touch. Any hour is fine
for maple syrup. Her husband stares
into a blue scattering of gulls, to forgive
himself toward a house he cannot
measure. The roof is off that place.

2

The park had been left to the animals,
and we walked in through a locked
gate as if into a chamber. But it was
only fog. There was a lockdown on
and four of us walked in through
the brume, a convocation of eagles
in attendance, wing-wide, curious,
no one else on the beach.
Her husband arrived on a bike,
and together we walked toward
whatever was now locked away.
One carried a small boat he'd
fashioned for the occasion. Two
carried flowers. One carried a song.
One carried her ashes. We circled up
on the beach, the tide ebbing, the better
to carry her out, the rook circling
our ankles, and we had a song,

a poem, a prayer, some ashes.
All she would need. Offered them.
Were strangely elated. Ran along
the shore chasing the ash-boat
as the tide took it out and out and
pulled her bier past the surf, past
the islands of the Salish Sea. A boat
with her ashes, a white sail that
showed itself on the dark interior
of the sea now and again.

in memoriam, Kathy Francis

SUSAN LEOPOLD FREEMAN
SALMONBERRY

There are two things that motivate me and ground me: the ability to create and the power I feel from the natural world. The first drives my commitment to working in pen and ink, oils, and mosaics. The second draws on the influence of my grandfather, Aldo Leopold, and plays out in my family's work to restore the salmon stream featured in our book *Saving Tarboo Creek*. Both my art and my connection to nature are core to my heart and life. So for me, a good day combines the two – whether it's sitting outside doing a pen-and-ink sketch, painting a floor cloth with bright plant forms, or spending the afternoon walking Tarboo Creek with friends to plant willow stakes and soak up inspiration.

TESS GALLAGHER
WRITING FROM THE EDGE: A POET OF TWO NORTHWESTS

I begin to think I am sometimes trying to
catch up to what has happened in a time
that hasn't happened yet.

One outreaches language in poetry when the in-seeing elements of consciousness ask the unseen of life to come forward. My aim has been to unseat what we assume about time, about the verities of love and death, of the consciousness of those other sentient beings next to us on the planet. We must put aside the glib assumptions we make just to domesticate our walking-around days.

The kind of poetry that seeks a language beyond the very one in which it arrives may travel from edge to edge. It is provisional and can't be too fussy about its sometimes awkward transport. In this pursuit, I find myself trying to out-leap what I can *almost* say — but that, if said outright, would utterly spoil the secret cargo that must somehow halo what is attempting to be given. I have even said that at this stage I seem to be writing in some sense *beyond language.*

I want my worlds to interpenetrate — for sky to merge with water, for fish and birds to exchange habitations so we re-experience them freshly and feel our differences, our interdependence, our kinships.

Drucilla Wall, in her essay on my work in *Thinking Continental,* hits on a central notion of my poetry when she quotes Vincent van Gogh from an epigraph in my 2011 volume *Midnight Lantern.* Van Gogh writes: "The earth has been thought to be flat . . . science has proved that the earth is round . . . they persist nowadays in believing that life is flat and runs from birth to death. However, life, too, is probably round." This possibility telegraphs an involvement with what Wall defines as my pursuit of "an ultimate elusiveness of meaning that permeates the concept of that non-linear roundness of life, alongside the simultaneous sense of living on the edge of everything in the West."

What she sees accurately is my attempt to bind up my two Northwests: their animals, my neighbors, Lough Arrow in County Sligo in the Northwest of Ireland with the high ridge of Bricklieve and its Neolithic passage graves reaching out to America and the Strait of Juan de Fuca, the snow-covered Olympic Mountain range behind Port Angeles, Washington. My fifty-year connection to the dead of Ballindoon graveyard merges with my haunting of my late husband Raymond Carver's gravesite at Ocean View Cemetery, west of Port Angeles, where I walked every day for two and a half years while writing *Moon Crossing Bridge,* that elegy to love and loss and ongoing gifts. . . .

The complexity of a poetry that seeks to deliver liminal space and time, that which occupies a stance at both sides of a boundary or threshold, has lifted me out of easy categories as a poet. I like Wall's locating phrase for me as having "an edge-of-everything sensibility." She posits further that if we go far enough, edging out and onward from the West, we end up in the East, that extension into the round.

My poems' ways of seeing do devolve from Eastern notions of reality. That is, they challenge dualities which tend to blot out a range of possibilities. Also, I adopt the Buddhist notion that each action we take bears importantly on the fabric of the whole, that the smallest creature, even a snail, has import – that all life is sacred and to be honored, that our path reveals itself according to our mindfulness of others and being able to see into the interconnectedness of choices.

Daily meditations, taken from a lifetime of reading Buddhist thinkers and religious leaders, are helpful to opening my mind in un-programmatic ways. One book usually in my bag as I cross back and forth between Ireland and America is *Openness Mind: Self-Knowledge and Inner Peace through Meditation*. The book is defaced with passages underlined and circled. "Try to develop a feeling for the thoughts watching the watcher"; below this I've scribbled the title of a poem I wrote later, "Little Inside Outside Thought." Or there is a question underlined in black ink: "But is there actually any 'now'?"

The seeming urgency of *now* makes it useful as a stimulus to actions which may, however, be shorn of important connections to before and after. When we consider now in the round of time, it is best experienced as a planet we are swiftly falling away from, but that we might re-encounter in a poem. Poems compress and expand time until the notion of *now* regains dimensionality. Such an idea of the "now" can have a past and future. It doesn't have to navigate only in the present.

Wall mentions ley lines of energy that are said to run through the very place in Ireland where I live, energy lines that are connected perhaps from Sligo's sacred sites to places as far away as the pyramids. She introduces the Irish term *dindsenchas*. The word means "a totality of topography, history, ecology, animal life, non-human life, spirit beings, and human impact on a place – *all the living and the dead in a non-linear simultaneity of presence.*" This passage delighted me – to discover there was already an Irish word for this complex notion of existence with which I'd been quietly working. This beautiful word carries forth a kind of poetic version of Einstein's relativity theory. It helps us stay in the round, in the deep mind I'd been drawn to in Ballindoon – for I had not stumbled upon it, but rather accepted its invitation.

When I visited the Buddhist nun Jakucho Setouchi in Kyoto in 1989 after the death of my husband Raymond Carver, she took me into her temple where she gave her legendary talks to women thwarted in love. We had instant rapport as if we had always known each other. "Why am I here?" I suddenly asked at one point, feeling as if some strong, beguiling force was at work. She answered, "*Because the spirits of this place have asked for you.*"

. . . A factor that joins my two Northwests is the dependability of rain in each. I yearn for it if I am deprived of it. My sensibility seems to need it as some painters crave the color blue. I also love gazing toward the west at sundown from my Sky House or Bay St. House in Port Angeles, for there is a wide sweep of sea between America and Canada. This sea view is always changing – one minute glassy, the next white-capped by wind. Cargo ships from China and Japan, cruise ships, and tug boats pass back and forth to Seattle or to the Pacific, and a ferryboat to Victoria, Canada, sails several times a day.

There is indeed a sense of being on the edge, the edge of the Pacific Ocean, which sends the orca whales through our strait and salmon to spawn and die in rivers fished for hundreds of years by the local tribes. When I was growing up on the Olympic Peninsula I was aware of five of the eight tribes in the area who had fished these rivers and ocean waters for hundreds of years: the Lower Elwha Klallam, the Quinault, the Hoh, the Quileute and the Makah.

The spirits of the American Northwest pulled me into small fishing boats with my father on the ocean from the age of five. Fishing teaches patience and the unknown, the unseen. Light illuminates the mind on water and the motion of the boat is a lullaby. It is a natural state of meditation. Speech on deep water is changed and intimate. The mind drifts. Things of a trivial nature lift away. Life seems bared to essentials. When one is on the ocean, one feels in touch with sacred space and non-linear time, that wistfulness toward simultaneity of times and places.

My childhood was spent in the logging camps where both my mother and father made our living, she as a choker-setter and he as a spar-tree-rigger. While my mother and father were felling trees, I was exploring with my brothers, building shelters, making trails, picking wild berries, tracking bear and deer. I was also always on the verge of getting lost in the greater forest.

It was all perhaps a preparation for becoming a poet – surrounded by the unknown, daring to venture, to pass back and forth from the wild to the domestic of home and hearth, all the while watching the larger-than-life efforts of my parents as they risked their very lives to earn a living from the forest.

Being with forests and oceans allows one "extremes of other-than-human domains." Wall says these connections in my poetry offer "a radical form of empathy that is not simply local and not absently, abstractly global."

In these exchanges, passing back and forth between my two Northwests, I leave hummingbirds and eagles in Port Angeles for goldfinches, mute swans, and wild pheasants in Ballindoon. I leave deer, black bear, cougar, and bobcats on the Olympic Peninsula for badgers, foxes, and elegant stags with their regal racks of horns in the West of Ireland.

I assume some cross-pollination of empathy and attentiveness must be taking place through bringing these disparate inhabitants together in one consciousness. In the process, and through my poems, I feel I am being transformed from the inside out.

ABBEY COTTAGE AND SKY HOUSE

Excerpt from the afterword from Is, Is Not (*Graywolf Press, 2019*)

IRENE KELIHER
WILD BLACKBERRIES

It is a treasure hunt and a battle, a dance and a game. I search for my quarry in thickets of grass, on crumbling tree stumps, and amidst dense English ivy, which is invasive, or woody salal, which is native and just as tough. On a green July afternoon I walk slowly down the quiet roads of my hometown, scanning the ditches and the underbrush. The Northwest sun filters through the maples and cedars; the air is still. Everyone else is at the beach or the country store for ice cream. I bend down to run my fingers along the bottom of an overgrown laurel hedge. There, a tangle of slim whitish vines. Here, a purple clump half-hidden by leaves.

As a girl I spent countless hours in these woods. I had favorite spots: a damp hollow behind a fallen tree, where I could read or pretend to be a pioneer; a thicket of sword ferns that provided good cover during hide-and-seek; the marsh near my cousins' house, full of salmonberries and sneaky river otters. Indianola remains small, but then it was even smaller; the trees stretched more or less unbroken from behind my house to the crest of the hill, and beyond that through federal tribal land, all the way down to the north peninsula coast. Seattle lies across the Puget Sound, just close enough to make a long commute there feasible, but when I was growing up, it always seemed worlds away. Indianola belonged to me. It was possible to spend days devoured by its trees, emerging only for snacks. The forest was forgiving, in its impartial way, and it was safe. The woods were a sanctuary, the berries a gift freely given.

It takes most of a day to gather enough berries for even a single pie. On Loughrey Street – the gravel part of it, just where it bends – I climb up a bank, having spotted a bunch of tiny, wild berries in the mess of ivy. I find more clusters beneath overlapping leaves. As is often the case, the visible berries are harbingers of a greater, hidden bounty. The ripest ones fall into my hands, unresisting. These, I eat: they're too soft to keep, and too sweet to ignore. To bite into one of our little wild blackberries is to encounter the intense, wine-rich flavor of the forest during the summer. I have eaten fresh mangoes in Nicaragua, roasted hazelnuts in Spain, and avocadoes straight from the tree in California, but none of these compare to my wild blackberries. I come home to visit so that I can search them out. They taste like the sun, damp earth, and honeysuckle, and like none of these things. They taste like home.

***

This wild blackberry is officially the species *Rubus ursinus,* Latin for "bramble bear," so named because bears love to snack on it. It's also known as the trailing blackberry and the Pacific dewberry, among other monikers. Widespread from British Columbia to California, the wild blackberry isn't harvested commercially, but it is the progenitor of the better-known marionberry and loganberry.

My family is not the first to prize the trailing blackberry. Native Americans throughout the region ate it fresh and dried into pemmican, or steeped the unripe fruit for tea. Its name in Lushootseed, the original language of many area tribes, is gʷə dbixʷ, and July was known as the month of the blackberry. My hometown sits on the Port Madison Indian Reservation, seat of the Suquamish Tribe. It is the smaller of the two towns on

31

the reservation and is dominated by white families. Eddie Carriere, a prominent Suquamish elder, lives in a beachside home in Indianola; he also owns swaths of land above town. One summer he let my cousin and me pick trailing blackberries on some of that land, a horse pasture full of scratchy underbrush.

Hot and sweaty, we tied cut-open plastic milk jugs to our waists in the style of the old cedar picking baskets. It took less time than usual to gather the fruit, which proliferated in the dry grass and along the barbed-wire fences in great clumps. Afterward, of course, we made Eddie a pie. Eddie loves pie.

Growing up, I didn't know the berry's history, but I did have a strong sense of its unique character. I knew that it belonged to the land in a way that the Himalayan blackberry did not. The Himalayan berry is what most Seattleites picture when they hear "wild blackberry." Though its fruit is oversized and sweet, this invasive plant is the scourge of gardeners and conservationists throughout the region. Introduced by famous botanist Luther Burbank in 1885, the Himalayan blackberry was prized at first for its abundant growth. It has since taken over the highways, parks, and alleyways of the West Coast and is now classified a noxious weed. It comes back with a vengeance unless its large, stubborn root system is completely removed.

I have a love-hate relationship with the Himalayan berries that congregate behind my house in southeast Seattle. The fruit has a mellow, juicy appeal that's synonymous with summer. Still, I'd take the taste of the trailing blackberry over the Himalayans anytime. I have thought of planting the little wild blackberry in my yard, but it seems incongruous. I don't imagine it would enjoy city life.

Rubus ursinus thrives in dense forest and clear-cuts alike. Indeed, the wild blackberry flourishes in "disturbed" areas. According to the US Forest Service, "it is particularly well represented following 'catastrophic disturbance' in Douglas-fir forests of the Pacific Northwest." After the eruption of Mount St. Helens in 1980, the trailing blackberry increased rapidly in the mudflow wasteland following the disaster. It was one of the first species to come back. *Rubus ursinus* is fundamentally wild. It doesn't bother with manicured lawns. It wants the woods, the dirt, and weeds. It finds its way onto scarred landscapes and thrives, satisfied to avoid scrutiny from all but the wildlife.

I think of this tiny berry as something unique to my childhood and town. It surprises me, when I do a Google search, to find that others admire it just as much. There is a foraging movement afoot in the Pacific Northwest, an outgrowth of the current obsession with all things local. Certain farmer's markets feature booths selling locally gathered mushrooms and greens, and high-end restaurants incorporate "wild foods" like trailing blackberries into their menus. I tend to view this movement with some suspicion. I assume its purveyors are of wealthier backgrounds than I am, or that they have grown up elsewhere and transplanted here along with so many other techies and foodies. But I have no idea. I'm probably just jealous.

It's easy for me to feel like a slight imposter in Seattle. From the moment I left home for my California college, I have lived with this dizzying sense that I don't belong where I have landed. This sensation has faded with time, but it has not gone away. As is to be expected, I suppose, it stays with me now even when I go home to Indianola.

I live about a mile from Seattle's iconic Seward Park. Occupying a small peninsula that juts into Lake Washington, much of it is covered by dense forest, where sometimes, when I wander up the interior paths and vanish into the deep green, I forget that I am in the city. There, I have seen wild blackberry vines, twining with familiar tenacity through salal bushes. These sightings give me a pleasant jolt of nostalgia. I never expect to see *Rubus ursinus* outside Indianola, illogical as this may be.

One day not long after making pie at my mother's, I leave the park and climb the steep hills westward to my house, which sits in a neighborhood that realtors might call "transitional." The fancier lakeside homes give way to more modest, middle-class dwellings, which in turn give way to rundown apartment complexes and medical marijuana dispensaries. It is a neighborhood of everyone: middle- and working-class black and white families, Vietnamese and Filipino immigrants, Latinos and East Africans, and even a sizeable group of Orthodox Sephardic Jews.

Here, I am choosing to raise my children and to put down roots. I pass the elementary school my sons will attend, the older brick homes, and the remodeled bungalows. Out of habit, my gaze follows the hedges and lawns, the occasional mess of grass, dandelions, and Himalaya blackberries. And then, just before I turn onto my street, I see them: *Rubus ursinus* vines, winking at me from the shrubs.

I kneel down, feeling gently for the fruit and tugging a few berries free. They tumble into my palm, a familiar shape and weight. It can't be, I think, but here they are. I lift them to inspect their color and I tear up, for a moment, for reasons I can't quite name. Just as quickly, I feel a bit silly and hope the neighbors won't notice me digging in the weeds.

I slip the berries into my mouth. The first is almost too sour to eat, and I wince. The rest are sun-warmed and sweet, nearly melting into juice. They all carry the taste of my childhood forest on a summer day.

This little wild blackberry, I am reminded, belongs to no one. It can grow anywhere it likes. It is free to do as it pleases.

ANA MARIA SPAGNA
SUPPLE

For few days each summer, I used to work in a small shop run by a cooperative of local artists, loosely defined. Kids sold whittled sticks and polished rocks. Adults sold birdhouses, ceramic bowls, knitted hats, and note cards, clever and original gifts that took time to craft. I sold books, and so took a few shifts behind the desk, and mostly talked to visitors who were, inevitably, less interested in the items for sale than the place where they'd landed, this lovely, narrow valley tucked in the North Cascades.

Their questions were predictable: Do you live here? Yes? How long have you lived here? Really, that long? What is winter like? If the first two questions annoyed me vaguely – as though I needed to prove my bonafides – the third delighted me. I'd turn and point to a black-and-white photo on the wall. Framed in barn wood, the photo showed snow piled four to five feet high in a local apple orchard. Each time I turned, my mood softened to near swoon.

Our first winter in the valley, thirty years ago, Laurie and I housesat for friends at the homestead in the orchard where the photo was taken. We borrowed gear and skied among aging apples trees, broke trail through tall firs to the river. We returned to the woodstove and played Dylan over and over on a turntable, and the scratchy voice, the scratched records, the scratch of snow-heavy limbs on the roof, all of it felt magical. Out in the orchard, snow converged in the vees where the limbs met the trunk, growing huge and splotchy until, after a while, the trees themselves looked made of snow.

I had long been enamored of the Pacific Northwest, but after that winter, I was hooked. I dug in to stay, apprenticed myself to trail work, to wet wool, to draw knives and peaveys, to making things that took time, and to paying attention, too, to the smell of damp duff, the trill song of a veery, the way cottonwood will dull a saw, the way white dogwood flowers curl brown in late June, how kokanee arrive just when larch limn the ridgetops and autumn light draws a slanted bead.

And then, then the snow!

It'd stick by Thanksgiving and stay until Easter. We skied and skied – I found a fast pair of waxless Fischers in a dumpster that would last me decades – and shoveled and skied. We walked on firm crust with the moon glinting on hoar frost. One year I dunked in the river every month of the year just to prove I could. Sometimes snow became a pain, of course. Wet slabs stuck to the bottom of our skis like sheet cake. We lost three windshields to heavy chunks dropping from high limbs – three! And the weight of the snow in those vees of the apple trees? It threatened to topple them, so Laurie, who'd taken over caretaking the orchard, headed out midstorm armed with prop poles to knock them free. But winter never lost its sheen even as the years got buried in sugar, slush, grapple, corn, and rare wondrous powder.

Rare, rarer, and rarer still.

By the early oughts, you could see the change. We'd rise early to shovel before eight, the hour when, we joked half-seriously, flakes turned to rain. When early season snow melted fast in fall, we had floods. When we got too little over the winter, we had fires. People who came to the valley for a short time, then left, or stayed only for a few weeks each year, marveled at the natural disasters. They tell stories of smoke-for-a month or roads washed to bedrock with the kind of wide-eyed wonder that says, Can you believe it? We could. We've seen it so often.

I've always worried about how fierce allegiance to a place sometimes reeks of exclusion. I've also worried about how it inures you, turns resilience to a kind of blindness. When you no longer feel wonder, you can't recognize astonishing change.

Last fall, mid-pandemic, by happenstance or a more purposeful instinct – running away? seeking newness? – I landed a temporary job three thousand miles away in the North Country in way upstate New York on the edge of the Adirondacks, smaller, round-rock mountains that seemed to me very old. Deciduous trees carpet them famously. Ferns and fungi thrive below. Beavers reclaim every pond and brook; their lodges swell to the size of a shack we once lived in. The papery pink underside of birch bark? Marvelous!

We made friends who cleave to this place with familiar allegiance. Walking together at a safe pandemic distance, they've shown us muskrat push-ups and shaggy hickory bark. They've explained that Adirondack rock is old indeed – "basement rock," it's called – but the mountains themselves are new, rising slowly to the surface and beyond. When I'm with them, I see allegiance differently, neither as exclusion or blindness but as deep knowledge, hard-earned perspective, ease.

They also warned us of the cold. Twenty below zero. Sometimes fifty below. Don't you have warmer shoes? they asked. Better gloves? We stocked up on down and wool. We girded ourselves. Then, nothing. So far, it's been balmy. Thirty degrees. Twenty at night. Of course it might change tomorrow, and I will eat my words. My friends say it still might. They've seen it so often. Though we all know the truth about what we've seen and what we think we know: all bets are off.

It's early January, and we've seen a few flurries, but we're still waiting for serious snow. We wake before dawn and peek out into the streetlights. Any yet? Any? Snow is transformation. A workaday raindrop suddenly flutters and swirls. Flakes accumulate as abundance, then let loose as sustenance. Meanwhile, we live in anticipation, our longing tinged with fear – what if it doesn't come?

I think a lot these days about that first winter in the orchard. The Dylan song we listened to most often, I realize with delight, was "Girl from the North Country," a duet with Johnny Cash, a song of pining for a girl in a place he'll never see again. I feel the same ache – we all do, don't we? – for home, yes, but also for an easier, more stable time, real or imagined. The friend we housesat for, the orchard dweller, always ended his handwritten letters the same way: Stay supple. It's a good reminder this hard season. As changes accrue, we can lean into adaptation. If you're prose-stuck, you can try poetry. If you're forest-shackled, you can find the sea. If you're water, you can be snow, and vice versa.

I have a confession to make. I've been talking about "allegiance" – a term of derision or at best ambivalence – for what I feel in my bones for the Pacific Northwest and now feel budding for the North Country, and I think I've begun to understand why. Allegiance has limits – this place instead of that one, this landscape not that one – and a prideful kind of *knowing* that implies stasis, whereas what I feel is more dynamic and expansive, more like *wanting*. To see more, to do more, to understand more, to care more. What I feel, of course, is love. Love for all wild places and even those that aren't so wild. Love, with its potential to hold and transform is, like snow itself, astonishingly supple.

We have a tentative plan to ski in the woods this weekend with our new friends. Coverage is light, so we'll slip over exposed roots and scratch our skis on rocks while we tell stories and laugh and pretend not to notice. When we reach the river, we'll cradle hot cups of tea and shovel cracker crumbs in our mouths. We'll watch beech leaves that refuse to drop tremble tawny in the wind and, with any luck, tiny flakes spin slowly, one by one, toward the earth.

JILL McCABE JOHNSON
SEASONAL ROUND

If you look from the window of an eastbound flight from SeaTac Airport, or peer perhaps through the eyes of Raven high above the land, you can see America slip past, dappled and elusive under a whisper of cumulus. Tahoma looms high in the Cascade Range, and to the east spreads the kingdom of salmon, where the mighty Columbia runs dammed and gagged. Land of the Great Spirit, where ten thousand years of flood silt and soil get parceled, ploughed, and planted. For more than ten thousand years, Indigenous peoples have traversed the lands and waters of the Pacific Northwest. In annual migrations called Seasonal Rounds, Interior Salish followed the seasons, traveling by foot, canoe, and later horseback and car to sites that offer nettle in spring; berries in summer; mushrooms, salmon, and deer in fall; shelter in winter. Coast Salish harvested and dried seaweeds for salts. They pickled bull kelp and dried berry mash into fruit leathers to eat in winter. Medicinal herbs like the leaves of plantain weed helped calm the pain of bee stings, and Wapato corms relieved indigestion. Traveling to and from sites in the islands, the mainland, river mouths, and deeper inland, their common sense and experience told them that, by following their ancient routes and traditions, the land provides for all.

But common sense is not as common as we think. The late cultural anthropologist Clifford Geertz saw common sense as a cultural construct, customs formed by practicalities relevant to that culture. So when European Americans entered into this land, they brought their practicalities of sowing, grafting, rearing, and reaping close to a stationary home. Common sense told them that moving an entire village of people two to four times a year, sometimes more, was impractical at best, hazardous at worst. They could store more tools and accumulate more helpful household goods by staying put, with everything within reach.

Who needs all that? Native Americans might have wondered. They traveled light, unencumbered by the unnecessary. Theirs was a practice of paring down. Quality over quantity. A watertight basket, a reliable blade, and anyone can find a handy rock to pummel roots or macerate herbs. Further common sense told them it was foolish to attempt subsistence on a piece of land that only provided during part of the year and offered paucity the rest.

Those European Americans called themselves explorers and pioneers, but they now seem more like colonial settlers at best, and invaders at worst. To their worldview, the lands they surveyed looked unmanaged and therefore unoccupied. If they saw no one there at the time, it meant no one was ever there. If they saw evidence of forest fire or brush fire, they assumed it was the ravages of nature, not a controlled burn to clear pastures for camas root and grazing deer, staples of many diets. In her book Imperial *Gaze: Travel Writing and Transculturation,* Mary Louise Pratt calls theirs a gaze "whose imperial eyes passively look out and possess." And in fact, Alexander Ross, in his journals as an employee of John Jacob Astor's American Fur Company, on a somewhat ill-fated expedition into the Northwest Territories, strategized about which Northwest tracts to colonize first, noting, "however inviting may be the soil, the remote distance and savage aspect of the boundless wilderness along the Pacific seem to defer the colonization of such a region to a period far beyond the present generation." He touted the benefits of first establishing operations and communities in locales such as the verdant Willamette Valley and parts of the Upper Columbia, including Celilo Falls, now subsumed by dam waters, where he predicted the salmon would make a profitable export for foreign markets.

"Settling" the west has always been about the exploitation of land and labor. The drivers behind that exploitation shifted from Spanish, French, and British royals and aristocracy to land barons and industrial barons, trading one kind of imperialism for another. Treaty commissioners facilitated the exploitation by divvying up the land, including portions of the Columbia Plateau between the Cascade and Rocky Mountains, arbitrarily grouping Indigenous peoples into confederations of tribes and designating the more valuable lands to be ceded.

University of Washington Professor Emeritus and Director of Kwiáht, Russel Lawrence Barsh, writes, "Collective tribal ownership is a legal fiction, like the legal fictions that the Americas were legally vacant when Europeans first arrived, or that Indigenous Americans lacked fixed settlements, institutions, or laws." The commissioners perpetuated these fictions by categorizing people as belonging to geographically based tribal groups, so the U.S. could negotiate treaties and land rights with a few purported leaders instead of hundreds of families. Even though the prevailing practice in Europe when governments or regimes changed was that individual property owners kept ownership of their land, the Native people's individual and family property rights were not recognized. By 1888, nearly all the lands along the Columbia River went into private ownership in land grants to settlers. In certain areas, with certain treaties, Indians at least retained access rights and could continue fishing their historic sites. However, companies and individual owners asserted the land was their own and theirs exclusively. With barbed wire, bully tactics, and sometimes even the courts, they attempted to block access.

Colonial exploitation is not exclusive to the Pacific Northwest or even the Americas. It mirrors the exploitation by and disparities between landed gentry and those of lower socio economic classes – disparities that inspired revolutions throughout the world, from the late eighteenth century on. Many of the Indigenous peoples of the Americas had similar class-based systems. However, the use of resources was typically restricted to a tenet of "take only what you need," and wealth was often measured by how much was shared with others. Land with a profusion of sustainably maintained birds, fish, plant life, and ancient trees not only demonstrated a family's wealth but attested to the care and responsibility they showed for future generations.

Not everyone has shown such care and responsibility. The earth has limited supplies of minerals and metals used in everyday items like cell phones, solar panels, and electric car batteries. More and more species become extinct as carbon increases and habitat diminishes. Atmospheric physicist Dr. Adam Green says the answer is not an either/or on whether to adapt to the current situation or mitigate the damage. "We need to adapt to what we've already caused," he writes, "and we need to mitigate it, so it doesn't become even worse." The same might be said about the legacy of overexploiting lands and peoples in our country. Without laws to protect against overexploitation, greedy industrialists not only damage the earth today but steal resources from future generations.

What does the common sense of the combined cultures who inhabit these lands look like now? Can it include sharing equally in effort, access, and opportunity – to education, jobs, medical care, and nature? Can we honor differences and prioritize restoration of cultures and ecologies? Can we remove trash, pollutants, invasive species, obsolete dams, and anything else that hinders healthy ecosystems? We could reintroduce indigenous plants. Eliminate toxins and plastics. Demand compostable packaging. Take longer walks. Shorter showers. Make gifts instead of buying. Learn crafts before they become lost arts. Honor our ancestors and protect resources so people can continue to cultivate and roam these lands for at least another ten thousand years.

The Coast Salish term Kwiáht refers to a place kept physically clean and spiritually healthy. And while we might not practice seasonal rounds in the same way many Indigenous peoples have done in the past, we can still allow access. Great Britain and much of Europe have secured access to natural places by enacting laws that guarantee rights to traverse historic trails and pathways regardless of property ownership. Water follows seasonal rounds that cleanse and replenish the land – clouds bring water inland, snow to mountains, spring thaws rush down rivers that in turn sustain mammals, insects, reptiles, and birds. The salmon we cherish like minor gods in the Northwest carry roe upstream. The spawning salmon die to feed their offspring. These gifts of water, deliverance, sacrifice, and sustenance all make their seasonal rounds. And so can we.

SANDRA JANE POLZIN
THE TIME BETWEEN

I may be the end of my ancestral line. I created this story map to reveal a slice of my ancestry, giving me a place to unfold memories because I need to keep the story alive. This is a map of my grandmother's journey from her village in the Nass River valley to Seattle aboard the *Princess Adelaide* in 1923.

SANDRA JANE POLZIN
KEEPING THE STORY ALIVE

In 1889 in the Nass River valley in British Columbia, my grandmother, Mary Amelia, was born into Laxgibuu (wolf) clan, a hunting and gathering clan, in the Tseax valley, Aiyansh village. She was the granddaughter of Chief James Woods and Jane of the Nisga'a Nation and the daughter of Nisga'a Jane Woods and German immigrant sailor FWB Elstermann. She was born in a time of waning interdependence on salmon, halibut, deer, seal, waterfowl, shellfish, and oolichan (smelt) and waxing European colonization, commerce, missionaries, and boarding schools.

In 1896, when she was seven, Mary Amelia was placed in an Industrial Boarding School for "Indian girls" in Metlakatla, where she stayed until she was sixteen, taking required instruction in sewing and cooking. She helped seasonally at Lawyer Island Lighthouse where Elstermann was the keeper from 1905 to 1922, tending the farm, harvesting shellfish, hunting, and shoveling snow. Boats of all sizes made it possible to motor to her seamstress position in Prince Rupert and millinery shopkeeper job in Port Essington, known for boardwalks where the tide ebbed and flowed under pilings and river ice floes halted travel.

In 1913, Mary Amelia married Leonard Dewhurst, a Marconi Telegraph engineer from England. Together, they homesteaded 124 acres on Porcher Island. There, Mary Amelia gave birth to two girls, fished, hunted deer and waterfowl, tended the gardens, and canned food.

In 1923, when Mary Amelia was eight months pregnant with her third daughter, she sailed with her three-year-old and seven-year-old daughters aboard the steam ship *Princess Adelaide* from Prince Rupert to Seattle, where she joined her husband. A series of misfortunes, lack of employment, three evictions, and Dewhurst's early death at fifty-three led Mary Amelia to start her own seamstress business. Once again, she fished, clammed, picked berries, and canned food for her family.

In 1941, Mary Amelia became a US citizen. Her daughters put their school and careers on hold, took jobs, and eventually purchased a permanent home for her. In 1979, Mary Amelia passed away, having lived a long, loving and resilient life.

Granddaughter Sandra Jane
Enrolled in the Nisga'a Nation, Laxgibuu clan since 2005

RENA PRIEST
REMEMBERING TA TA AT T'AM WHIQ SEN

A glossary of bell related words chimes,
sings, peals, tolls… It is a feeling of silver.
It rings and shines at the edges.

Like the scales of a fish, it flickers,
tintinnabulates the signal of a charm,
of magic, of a movie memory sequence,
and then, there is mother,
home from the cannery, covered
in the scales of hundreds of gutted fish.
She shimmers like a mermaid.
"Long day?" I ask.

"When I lunch at noon," she replies,
"the sky is a polished silver spoon.
By quitting time, tarnish
has overtaken all signs of shine.
That's how long the day is."

"You must have cleaned a lot of fish." I say.

"I think we cleaned out all of Puget Sound…
There used to be gooseberries
at Gooseberry Point.
Now there is the cannery.
Won't be long
before all the fish are gone,
then the cannery will go,
and all we'll have is hunger
and sorrow."

A bourdon is the heaviest bell
of a carillon. Its register is low.

I wish I had a magic wand
to chime the cheerful sound
of gooseberries sprouting up,
out of the ground.

RENA PRIEST
(A POEM IS A) NAMING CEREMONY

What has grown out of what has gone away?
The clear-cut patch has grown larger on the mountain.
The rivers have grown murky with timber trash
and there's enough runoff manure to grow corn
out there on the tide flats.

I don't want to think about what has gone away.
I want to meander and play and forget myself
until I can grow a new me in place of all this grief —
learn the language to see the cotton wood
as kwealich ich, the dancing tree;
the killer whales as qwel' lhol mechen,
our relatives under the sea,
the whole glorious landscape
filled with meaning to end my grieving.

When I was young, I was invited to learn
Xwilngexw'qen, the people's language,
but I said no. I didn't understand. I thought
I wanted to learn how to be rich. I didn't know
the only way to possess all the wealth of the world
is by naming it — here is birdsong, here is the kiss
of a lover, here is the feel of cold water at the peak
of summer . . . I have spent my life with words,
trying to name a hint of what I lost by not
learning my language. Estitemsen. Tu totest sen.
Estitemsen.

ANN SPIERS
ENZO: OPEN, CLOSED

The flush landscape disappears
in a push of erasures leaving
an alphabet of sticks and spaces
to reassemble in the slot
between greyed dawn
and sunset's muting of light.

Rain freezes mid drop.
My gloved hand pulls
the newspaper from its box
roadside. The walk back
takes months of nothing.

Feverfew
broken in my fingers,
and Scotch-broom pods
pop in the odd heat.
Last game: my turn up at bat.

From the old man's orchard,
we all steal apples. Maggots thread
the flesh with brown silk.
White buckets wait at the fence.
Shadow pushes sun.

Strapped to her gurney,
Cassiopeia is left on stage,
a fistful of stars smudged
in the smoke of a hard day's night.
The West is on fire.

Our last swim through herds
of jellyfish. Moons they are,
their gonads thickening orange,
bumping us, their glisten
sliding over and under.

We burn fists of soft rush,
mix ash and water for ink.
Our letters ascend and descend.
The letter O slows our progress:
perhaps a circle closed, or open
if we lift the brush, relenting.

ANN SPIERS
THINGS FALL APART

Shi Shi Trail

On our return, we eat amid a surfeit
of salal berries, purple ink, skins
sticky, pitchy, spaced on a stem.

Satiated, our appetite slides to curiosity.
We finger open the berry, seed triparted
like the Trinity – Father, Son, and Holy Spirit.

A spider, minute, muddling ripe flesh,
picking out space within, lifts its articulated
legs against our nails opening its nursery.

A worm, white, segmented, eye dot,
contracts its length, curves upward,
its head swaying against our probing.

We've consumed more than berries.
We eat God's creatures, each
in the berry to deposit larva,

and those soft things feed off
the swash of sweet. They harden, emerge,
Arachne herself or wings unfolding.

We hear *the center cannot hold,*
our world disordered at our sundering
the berry, our vast appetite, our curiosity.

BETHANY REID
HOW IT FALLS

Let it all fall sometimes.

~Rose Cook

This year, it's not only the leaves that fall.
After pandemic and lockdown,
murders and protests, and now
elections looming, the year itself
seems to collapse with an exhausted whoof,
a tent in a finished carnival,
rusted mechanisms dismantled
and packed away. School begins, or not,
another sort of fall,
innocence refusing to give way to experience.
Temperatures fall, and rain.
Light falls, tumbling down
playground slides without children.
Starlings startle, rising up, banking together,
then they, too, are falling, scattering
across the trampled grass.
In the fall of this year, like every other,
you must learn to trust like a parachutist
in harness, to have faith if not in religion
then in the balloon of the chute
lowering you to the falling earth.
You must open your arms to what follows
from falling. You must become the fall.

Ronda Piszk Broatch
Apologizing for Paradise

Surrounded by birdsong in many languages
walled in by forty-, fifty-, sixty-foot cedar, fir, hemlock
maples leafed out, honeysuckle beginning

its evening release of scent, geranium burning red
all day long. Somewhere a police officer presses
his knee into the neck of a Black man who will take

nine minutes to die. Sometimes a bee finds respite
on my sweatshirt, flies off, returns over and over.
There is no paradise like this one,

the way morning sun filters through large pink poppies,
the yellow bells of daylilies open to hummingbird.
How the raven and crows mimic the sounds

of water, of wood. And who is going to tell
his children he loves them, his momma, his breath
denied him while bystanders witness,

hold up their phones like damning flames.
There is no paradise like this one, swallowtails gathering
nectar from lilac. What is native, fern and foxglove,

take hold here, cotton drifts on wind that keeps at bay
the narrative outside the gate. And there is no paradise
for the ones left behind, no fire-blazing sun enough

to bring to justice, no lilies and lilacs and swallowtails,
bees, ferns, and poppies enough to stave off hatred,
its roots so impossible to spade. Somewhere,

this story repeats itself. Even in paradise
it can be hard to breathe. Figs swell beneath leaves
spread like hands meant to protect them.

K'EHLEYR MCNULTY
UNPRECEDENTED

They say we're living through unprecedented times

Not me though, I've been here before

When the news roared louder than the wildfires

Folks began to panic, choking on their fear

Not us though, we've seen this all before

Strange, primitive beings emerged all over town

Humans with eyes hollowly ablaze

Mine alight with a deep knowing

Shortage of food

Shortage of toiletries

Shortage of rational acts

They strayed further apart, every man for himself

We communed, began to hunker down

No strangers to this intruder

"Unprecedented, like nothing we've ever seen"

Well, aside from 1918

I laugh heartily at their short memory, then grimace

There is blanketed loss to come

"Stay in, wear a mask"

DO NOT GATHER

"NO!" they defiantly cry

Crocodile tears for freedoms never tethered

We share stories, share love, share in mourning;

Cousins - Elders - Knowledge dying

Phase one. Phase two. Phase three.

Eat, drink, be merry

Relish in your economy!

And they did

And they died

And they're dying

Maybe next time,

Their bones will warn them

Reminding them that this is familiar

Certainly nothing

Unprecedented

MARY MORGAN
FAN TAN ALLEY

Last January
Just a ferry's ride from here
We visited another world:
Horse-drawn carriages, charming tea shops,
A rowdy Irish pub,
And Chinese noodles for lunch.

Around the corner and two doors down
Fan Tan Alley lured us in.
Incense and dampness filled the air.
Echoes of voices
And beams of winter sunlight
Mingled with shadows and
Bounced between high brick walls.
Crystals, scarves, pipes, and jewels
Cluttered the windows of tiny shops.

Just an in-between place
Wide enough for two.
A bright red door,
Number 23 1/2.

We can't get there now.
The ferry shut down,
Borders closed,
The virus circling.

Here we are suspended,
In a narrow place.
Lights, shadows,
The people we love,
All that we hope for
Echoing, bouncing
Between the walls.

ELIZABETH AUSTEN
MAY

to the juncos

on the day we cross
the 100,000 mark

I offer to your black hoods
unconditional surrender

here   eat   here bathe
only endure   we can't go back

can't unstack the errors
one friend drives five hours

to see the father who kept
his chest pain secret nearly a week

sure he'd only lifted his wife into bed
one too many times   another friend

moves out of the apartment she and her
wife shared until infidelity surfaced

again like a weed with infinite roots
this was merely days after a policeman

murdered George Floyd with his knee
his hands in his pockets   offering

a smirk to the cameras   I'm orchestrating days
to a score I can't decipher   no one is in charge

what will be reckless
in retrospect

I rinse my hands   rinse again
hair and thoughts

equally unkempt   I fever
my gaze to the window

like a lover craving hourly
rendezvous   envy

your untroubled habit
your forage   flock   flight

51

JENIFER BROWNE LAWRENCE
REFLECTION AT SUMMER SOLSTICE IN THE MIDDLE OF THE PANDEMIC

In the mirror my hair is unruly but light shines through it,
sparse waterfall against a green hillside deep in the Hoh Rain Forest.
Pockets of daylight filtered strand by strand. You could say this untamed mane
is the resilience of late middle age. From the world mirror,
arriving in time for the new year, this knobby sphere —
tinted red, bouncing out and retreating like a paddle ball
on elastic string. For the one-hundred-seventh day I back away
from the crowned conqueror. Oh, that's novel, we say, a new organism!
So tiny, so determined! Ubiquitous disco ball casting dance light
everywhere, twirling unseen through regulated air.
I cover my face with black cloth, I cover the mirror. COVID-19,
though we have not met I imagine you float over the threshold,
winged royalty, joker, trickster, and king.
I want to defend without genuflection.
To forestall, deflect, to practice inspiration.
To breathe without begging.

To breathe without begging.
To forestall, deflect. To practice inspiration,
I want. To defend without genuflection,
winged royalty. Joker, trickster, and king,
though we have not met I imagine you float over the threshold.
I cover my face. With black cloth, I cover the mirror. COVID-19
everywhere, twirling unseen through regulated air
so tiny. So determined, ubiquitous. Disco ball casting dance light
from the crowned conqueror. Oh. That's novel, we say. A new organism
on elastic string. For the one-hundred-seventh day I back away,
tinted red. Bouncing out and retreating like a paddle ball
arriving in time for the new year. This knobby sphere
is the resilience of late middle age. From the world mirror,
pockets of daylight. Filtered strand by strand, you could say. This untamed mane,
sparse waterfall against a green hillside deep in the Hoh Rain Forest.
In the mirror my hair is unruly, but light shines through it.

ARIANNE TRUE
PANDEMIC: EVEN THE NICE DAYS, WE'RE INSIDE

The forest drifts in through the window, rising up the slope
      from narrow water carving low points lower.
Once with you, a wading bird we watched,
              waiting to see how close it would
come. Now that trail is gated by the threat of breath, too many
      people too close, path sated and spilling over.
         I am hungry for the touch of ferns,
             for happenstance and a lost world of
coincidence I once felt standing all around me,
         like a stand of trees in the city

KELLI RUSSELL AGODON
POEM WHERE THE LAST LINE IS THE TITLE

Today we grew wild
strawberries, read poetry in a garden
of birds – blue jays, winter hawks,
your hand cradling a greenfinch
because a breeze blew it from its nest.
How can we breathe when life is so quicksilver,
such quicksand in our cartoon lives? Today we grew
stronger, the firepink blooming over your shoulder
made me lean into the sky, socially distanced
from Jupiter, all red-lipped and strawberry stained.
And when the kingfisher hovered, I thought –
We will never capture what is wild. Nor should we
want to. Let the skittish herons never be bored
with the thin silver fish darting past them.
Let life's colors never fade even as we don't
call a redo of this day, instead rediscover
the sunset in our cheeks,
a time we once called *normal.*

Jessica Gigot
Two Mothers Walking

for Anna

We thought they were swans.
Far offshore in a huddle,
lazy swans that chose
to stay.

But the long arc of orange
gave them away. Stragglers,
climate change refugees
that in a normal year
would never reach
our northern cove
of coastline.

But what is normal anymore?

We were talking
about life and babies. My
daughter, about to walk.
Your daughter, graduating.

You want to clutch
and hold her close, while
mine refuses to be put down.

They grow up so fast, you say.
I need more time to myself, I say.

Driven to near extinction by pollution
these pelicans are a miracle.
                    Or an omen.

We stride slowly, like the unfurling tide
acknowledging these visitors
            and the fierce uncertainty
of what may come next.

SKYE LEVARI
DOWNWIND, WILDFIRE

Through the skylight, the thick haze
resists the sun and orange sepia
wrestles into the house, density
distorting depth perception.

Here, it is smoke, it is fine particles of ash,
claustrophobic scenery. Windows shut,
and somewhere else flattened homes
and whole stories, forests turned grey

with heat. Neighborhoods carved empty
as the word *evacuate* moves into
adrenaline-packed bodies. Here, nothing
changes except maybe the lungs.

Craving the breadth of feeling,
anything besides faces full
of dissociation. Which is to say:
capitalism tunnels into the soft

flesh of the body and we wake
downwind, blue in the face with grief,
climbing into the day, normal.

SHARON HASHIMOTO
BACK FIRES: SEPTEMBER 2020

We sulk in the basement. Outside, smoke
hangs like a veil, a scarf we can't breathe through,
turning the sky orange-red. Our eyes dry out
from staring at scenes on the screen of flames
spreading in the forests. We're the bunkered
survivors of an apocalypse. Only back fires,
we're told, seem to slow the advance of char.
I remember the childhood lesson of tree rings –
if a hemlock survives, the cat face burn
at its base will mark the year of growth.

Years ago, with me in a pink raincoat,
my father guided my steps through the rain
over moss-covered logs. Some were so thick
I could ride a fallen fir like a horse, the wet
seeping through the legs of my pants. Cold
slowed my frozen fingers as a long stick
I walked with poked the earth for Japanese
pine mushrooms. I couldn't tell the sweat
from dew gathering on my bangs. In my misery,
I loved the scent of woods and water.

Back in my dry, overheated body, I stare
at the firefighters on the news bending
with the wind. What will survive? Burn morels,
those mushrooms poking their tops through the earth
and mistaken for pine cones, will fruit
for a short while. My father five years gone,
I'm glad he died and missed this, his ashes spread
into Commencement Bay. In the old house, with only
the picture of my mother and the crooked smiles
of his adult children on the wall, might Dad wonder
how much fire it would take to burn out
memory? My fingers clench as if to hold on
as I make a wish for the scarred forest.

SHARON HASHIMOTO
WASHINGTON COVID DEATH TOLL PASSES 2,700: NOVEMBER 2020

The coin of the sun sets and the bottom
of its orange-yellow melts into a stripe
spreading behind the Olympic Mountains.
One by one, starlings rise from roosting
to fly, the chevron of beating pinions
shape-shifting into a column, a rippling
Mobius strip that suddenly lifts up
into a scarf of bird-smoke. What makes
each individual dive-spin, veer, and return
as if belonging to one mind? Crows
mourn when one of their own dies.

We shout as we witness a meteor-shape
plummeting toward us, the caws and swaths
of wings vertiginous. The sight alarms
me – a pattern as erratic as the spread
of a disease. But I know the starlings
are not invasive, not strange to themselves.
The flock wheels together – every bird shifts
as the wind swings or at each swivel
among their seven nearest neighbors.
As we point and cry out, our crowd
draws together. We pull apart.

TINA SCHUMANN
October

Lately, it's been like Groundhog Day
around here; same thoughts, same steel
whistle of the kettle, same slow pulse
of another smoky sunset. Still, people
really are trying – what with their chipped
toothed jack-o'-lanterns
crouched on the front porch
and gauzy ghouls peeking out
the screen door. They are trying
to say hello to this misstep of a season
contained within this misstep of a year.
This close to the end of it all we reach out
for the usual and the comfort of a childhood
mask. As if the scare tactics of reality
were not enough. We want the kind of fear
we can decorate and fold away in a box
the next day. Now that we are all bipolar
and understatements abound – it's a trick
of the mind to keep going – a treat to be
delusional together. That's OK. Let's be something
less capricious than the garden variety delusional;
you buy the waxy candy bars in their little coffins
of colorful paper, and I'll screw in the red lightbulb
over the front door. Someone is bound to ring
our bell in their chosen disguise
just begging for something
completely different.

KATHLEEN FLENNIKEN
HORSE LATITUDES

A raft of debris as large as Africa
accumulates in the Pacific gyre —

trash, plastic, rope, netting — a synthetic sea
of flotsam that will outlive us all.

Few ships enter. A windless ocean
strikes terror in the crew.

If you can't imagine
the camera pulling back, pulling back

until we see the curve of the earth,
pulling back to reveal the atmosphere's

blue glow and still not bounding
the garbage — if we can't acknowledge

the damage done — then recall your secret hurt
that churns and churns and won't

diminish — a spiral so huge
your mind mutinies and denies it all.

KATHLEEN FLENNIKEN
SEVEN SEAS

The one we've fished to death,
that tosses ships till they sink,
so deep the fish at the fissures
squiggle instead of swim, glow
instead of gaze.

The one inside a conch shell
that sweeps us from the couch
to its shore – our first metaphor.

The sea of ones and zeros
with tributaries pressing Send,
where our secrets glitter
in the data gyre.

The sea of refugees, turned away, turned away, turned away,
crashing the razor-wire fence.

The sea of cash, thick
with trawlers' tangling nets, green
with the drowned and drowning.

The sea of regret
that surges and retreats
and sucks at our feet,
a tide that takes us nowhere.

And the final sea of liquid light
we'll only know from below.

Carolyne Wright
Triple Acrostic: Orcas

Why the pods that used to streak and shimmy
        in Puget Sound's granitic light
have disappeared in recent decades: the reasons
        speed like a killer Chris-Craft through clouded
inland waters. Reasons subtle as a buccaneer's
        logic: Goliath-girthed trunks of
Douglas fir that shadowed these estuaries
        and mussel-crowded coves – all felled
by axes that traveled ever farther up the temperate rainforest's
        northernmost reaches, their salal-shadowed mosses
exempted from protection by our bombast. In the global
        dance that warms to its own internal warnings, coastlines
yield like Roosevelt elk hides espaliered against a
              wall map of the illusory Northwest Passage –
              aquatinted waves where the shades of orcas frolic.

In memory of K7, a.k.a. Lummi,
leader of the Puget Sound K pod,
disappeared in December 2007
at about 98 years of age.

BETHANY REID
LAST LAMENT FOR 2020

When you are weary of grieving
the virus's mounting death toll, exhausted
by talking about the election, fed up
even with grieving your petty losses,
the restaurant closures, the stupid masks,
the locked churches and theaters,
you might make room to miss the splendid poison frog,
declared extinct in 2020, or the smooth handfish,
which appears on the same year's list of farewells,
though not sighted on the ocean floor since 1802.
With our songbirds dying by the millions,
it's foolish to go on too long lamenting your parents
who died in old age after long, happy lives,
pointless to sigh over friendships let go,
jobs poorly done, siblings who don't vote
the way you do. So life hasn't always treated you
to your fondest desires, why write about that,
when the northern white rhino
and the Tapanuli orangutan are about to blink out
of existence entirely? Is your own heart still thumping,
are your lungs drawing air? Give some thought
to the Jalpa false brook salamander
who has neither lungs nor heart left to it,
and the Bonis pipistrelle bat who will never again
go soaring out into the dark. Focus on the gap
left behind as the clock of all species gets wound tighter
and tighter. There is work to be done,
while you have hands to do it. If the poet's burden
is to name difficult things, bear in mind that naming
is also your joy. Hold to that joy,
even as your time here grows shorter,
even as you, too, prepare to say goodbye.

SHELLEY KIRK-RUDEEN
ZUMWALT PRAIRIE

The shadows of clouds race northward.
Above the shush of wind in pine and grass,
listen: timbers groaning,
the ark creaking to life.

This will be no gathering of two by two.
There will be no one place to call home.
Everything on the move, leaving
to become native to new places
as the old homes change,

traveling by windblown seed, by wing,
by cloven hoof and padded foot,
in bellies and in dung, in water's flow.

And what of the ones who travel
by rhizome's reach,
by the exquisite slowness of slime trail?

And what of the ones who must stay?
Is it only their names we will carry forward?

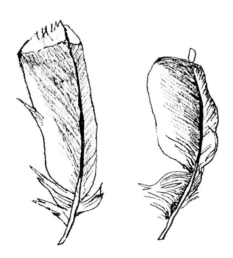

ALICIA HOKANSON
WORLD WITHOUT US

No one has told the gulls
the human world is doomed:
they scrabble loudly over the herring ball
roiling in the sun. But those two crows
crying as they strut the tideline this afternoon
give a piercing, inconsolable moan.

The sun doesn't know, nor the tide,
or the big combers rolling in to take out
the fire-ring rocks, flatten the beach,
and rearrange the logs. They will keep
thrashing the shore long after we are gone,
when the sea has moved a hundred feet up
into the trees and carved out a newer island.

Who will miss our loud machines
and brutal histories? Miss our beach chairs
and the shouts of children playing
in the shallows? Miss our tended gardens
and tamped roads connecting house to house?

The wrens in summer thickets will still
be here. And morning silence, I hope.

What of our words? Our small, thin songs
of praise or love? Leave them
to the whales. I hope the whales go on
carrying longing through the deep
watery canyons of the world.
And for the shore, the crow's dark lament.

RISA DENENBERG
FROM *POSTHUMAN*

We know we're unprepared for what's in store.
We won't be going home again. What was home
anyway? Wonder Bread and Log Cabin syrup?
Pabst Blue Ribbon and Twinkies? Or was it where
we learned that the birthday balloons we released
did not go to heaven; they killed turtles. We buried
pets in the backyard and fled across continents.
Too late I saw it was I who colonized, condoned
slavery, flattened Hiroshima. Our bodies contain
sewage, double lattes, oncogenes. We angst about
the planet, and fill our homes with shit. We plug
the ocean with plastic and expect lunch at noon,
milk and animal crackers at bedtime. Truth time.
We've committed the unforgivable and buried it.

*

I've committed the unforgivable. Once,
I swathed a stray cat in an old robe and buried her
in curbside trash. She prowled into my studio
to die nameless. Would it have been different
if she'd had a name? Isn't a dead body proof
enough? I've moved far from that walk-up
in the East Village, far as possible from those
memories. My home is now the PNW, where
I find churning yawns of rising oceans, refugees
drowned at sea, dry riverbeds gone to boneyards.
When strangers come calling, will I feed them?
Will I clothe the naked, comfort the sick, house
the homeless? It's too late to repent. Squalls
lurk nearby. Tsunamis loom at the horizon.

*

Who is drowning in plundering seas?
Who burns in the millions of acres blazing
from Arctic to Amazon? Who is bitten by
malaria-carrying mosquitoes newly arrived
in Texas, or mourns the last trumpeter swan's
disappearance from the tundra? "In the end,
the departure came without warning," Etty
Hillesum wrote. We've been warned. Before
her murder at Auschwitz, she said, "I don't
think I would feel happy if I were exempted
from what so many others have to suffer."
Of course, I'm unhappy too. Etty rebukes
me, "A hard day, a very hard day. We must
learn to shoulder our common fate."

The quotes from Etty Hillesum are from An Interrupted Life: The Diaries, 1941–1943 & Letters from Westerbork *(Henry Holt and Co., 1996). Etty Hillesum died in Auschwitz on November 30, 1943.*

ZANN JACOBROWN
THE PERSISTENCE OF KINDNESS

It was the beginning of the pandemic and a friend and I decided to chronicle it, she through poetry and me through a spontaneous form that mixes writing with drawing. It usually involves a several-mile meditative walk to notice what catches my heart, sketching it with watercolor pencils, and writing around it.

An old-growth stump sits at the base of a hundred-foot cliff of sand and clay by the Salish Sea, ringed by mountains, distant sailboats, and heavy freighters. It's a place I've come for thirty years for inspiration and solitude. This may not seem like a pandemic story, but it is. The massive stump rests with roots in the air, worn away by salt, time, and sun to reveal its bones, beautiful and expressive. During this disrupted, lonely, and anxious time, I thought this elder would have something to say. And she did.

PAULA MacKAY
A DROPLET OF WILD HOPE FROM THE EPICENTER

First the vibe changes. A city that prides itself on being chill suddenly becomes the hot zone, and your ears are on fire from the news.

Seattle's Patient Zero spreads virus.

First US death occurs in Seattle.

Seattle has turned into a ghost town.

Then the closures and cancellations reach epidemic proportions. Concerts. Conferences. College campuses. Public schools. Everybody work from home. Nobody is safe from COVID-19.

Your quaint little island, a ferry ride from downtown, feels a bit like a refuge – until it does not. One case. Two cases. Okay, here we go.

You sing happy birthday to your hands to make sure they're clean. You race through the market to stock up on food, buying extra bananas for your disabled twin. You call loved ones on the phone while you wipe down your groceries. You wipe down your phone, and also your dog, although you know the latter is probably silly. You practice social distancing – an oddly disquieting term you'd never heard until three weeks ago. You hug your husband, a lot. You swear that, tomorrow, you'll take a break from the internet. Mostly you worry. You worry about family, and older folks around town. You worry that you're no spring chicken yourself, despite your husband's kind words. You worry about your newborn grandniece in Boston, whose middle name is Hope. You worry that hope itself will go extinct.

The world is in chaos. Everything has changed.

And yet.

You walk in the woods, where skunk cabbages bloom their bright yellow hoods.

You lift tired fern fronds from a mat on the ground to find the fresh curl of fiddleheads emerging beneath.

You see the stalks of spring nettles growing free in your yard and think, *Oh, good! We can steam away the stingers and eat greens tonight.*

You hear the tuning-fork tones of varied thrushes at dawn and remember what sunshine feels like after a soggy Northwest winter.

You catch a familiar floral scent on the passing breeze and, for the life of you, can't recall its botanical source. *Who cares?* you tell yourself. *Just breathe it in.*

You schedule lunchtime strolls six feet from your friends, plant cucumber seeds in small fiber pots, replenish the birdfeeder for the second time today.

You stop on the road to say hello to your eighty-two-year-old neighbor, whose eyes still sparkle as he shuffles toward home. I'm taking walks every day, he says. What else can I do?

Your own eyes water with the flush of spring pollen and then, without warning, fill softly with tears. The trees keep on giving, and so must you.

From the beach near your house, you watch two bald eagles circle their nest – a tangle of dead branches that will soon brim with life. The eagles were soaring here last March, too.

You gaze across the sound at the Seattle skyline, which can seem almost tranquil from nine miles away. And beyond the tall buildings, the Cascade Range, a sinuous spine of solitude shedding its season of snow.

You imagine a black bear shaking loose from her torpor, her trio of cubs a chortling mob by her side.

You picture the gray wolves who have returned to this place, and the itinerant wolverines, wandering pathways of ice.

You can't wait to be out there again – in that big, lonely wild.

From the eagle's perspective, everything is the same.

If I had to tell you why Seattle is a literary city, I would say it is because I was able to become myself here. I learned how to inhabit my mind in this place. To hold space for your own story can be a revolutionary act.

The kindness and cruelty I have encountered in our region and history have compelled me to claim my own responsibility. When I first moved here in 2004, I became a reporter for the *Seattle Post-Intelligencer,* now gone. Hurrying around town to conduct interviews on deadline, worried about the game of chicken that we play on sideroads, I learned to cope with the dark, wet chill of our winters. I was born in a state as hot and humid as a person's mouth. Freed from hurricanes, I am haunted still by the specter of a subduction-zone earthquake. Keep what you'll need handy.

I didn't always expect disaster. They say anticipation is the greater part of pleasure, and maybe there is a sick edge to knowing it could soon be fractured, this city, and with it our fragile bodies, houses, psyches. I don't know how we tolerate the cognitive dissonance of planting our lives in unstable soil. Those who moved here chose our fate within a seismic reckoning which I've come to see as myriad. Not just geologic but cultural. Not just topographic but economic. Not just historical but immediate.

This place helped make me who I am. Like so many settlers before me, I aim to stay. No es fácil. Food and shelter cost so much that people go without and are blamed for it. This, too, is a reckoning we must face – the compression of oncoming waves of workers in diaspora, come to seek jobs that may not provide. And yet, provide we must.

As a UNESCO City of Literature, we carry stories for the unborn. What will we tell them of our time?

That in a pandemic we were asked to choose between profit and our vulnerable, elderly neighbors? That death forced us to keep a social distance? That to confront and heal our racial divides, we came together – or broke apart?

As editor of *Seismic: Seattle, City of Literature,* I asked artists and storytellers to reflect on what it means for Seattle to be a City of Literature. While celebrating Seattle's inclusion in the UNESCO Creative Cities Network, this collection is not a commemoration. It is a call to action. How can literary culture influence social change? *Seismic* is a living portrait of a city we love too much to lose.

The essays represent a vision for our city that channels the best hopes of its artists, who were asked for their opinions prior to the pandemic, and whose wisdom should be considered as we revitalize our city's neighborhoods and cultural institutions in the wake of COVID-19.

Reader of the present, take note: the reader of the future will study our society for clues about what and whom we protected. They will see whether we preserved and shared our abundance.

The corporate wealth which controls public process would have us believe anything is achievable if we work harder. A freelance veteran of the gig economy, I am here to tell you that such lies are designed to divest us of our labors. We are ceding control of the narrative. To what end?

Shall we tell them that ours was among the first generations to listen to women, and that when we spoke it was a howl?

That the earth spoke, and we did not listen?

We cannot answer these questions alone. Take strength in knowing that Seattle writers, readers, literary organizers, and activists have counterparts in Barcelona, Baghdad, Bucheon, Durban, Lviv, Melbourne, Milan, Nanjing, Odessa, Prague, Reykjavík and beyond. Together we can own up to our role in the long story of living. If the personal is political, then the local is global.

We, whether newly arrived to Seattle or generations deep, are on Duwamish land, now deforested and poisoned by the hands of forebearers who straightened rivers, sluiced hills and flooded shorelines in the name of prosperity that has not been shared. It is time to honor the Treaty of Point Elliott, signed in 1855 by Chief Si'ahl, our city's namesake. Native wisdom has lasted for millennia. And that is what UNESCO reaches for – the millennia, not just those which have already unfurled but those which remain for others to endure.

What must be remembered bears repeating. Resilience is a quality cultivated under duress, over time, against the odds and in community. To hold space for story is a sacred duty and a real joy in my literary life, in gratitude for which I remain,

Yours,
Kristen Millares Young

A free downloadable copy of Seismic: Seattle, City of Literature *can be found at www.seattlecityoflit.org/ seismic-seattle-city-of-literature.*

WENDY CALL
A PANDEMIC WITH PRECEDENT

On September 11, 2020, incinerated forests hang in the Pacific Northwest air, piercing my lungs, singeing my eyes, vise-gripping my skull. I go to the university campus where I teach writing – for the first time in six months. Since early March, I have taught my students via yellow-framed boxes on my computer screen, via endless words typed and read on my university's cumbersome online course system, via email messages. Today, I go to campus to leave books for my students – actual books they can touch and smell and write in and doodle on and stain with drips of coffee or soda or beer. Because most of the campus is empty and locked up tight, I must convince the campus security office to let me leave the stack of books on the ledge outside the Plexiglass shield that separates me from them.

***

When our spring sequestration bloomed into summer seclusion, I decided to spend my summer entirely at home. I love this place: a 110-year-old house on a South Seattle hill, halfway between the place where Chief Seattle's oldest daughter, Kikisoblu – called Princess Angeline by the white settlers – was born and the place where she lived her adult life. We usually spend as much of the summer as possible outside, but crowded campgrounds and hiking trails seemed too large a risk. My partner Aram and I bought two used kayaks – the most socially distant, close-to-home summer escape we could imagine.

We improvised a kayak-carrier roof rack out of pieces of foam rubber, old yoga mats, bungee cords, and duct tape. We drove our old car gingerly down the hill toward the water to launch into Lake Washington, from the park that the Suquamish people called "Taboo Container," a place believed to be home to a malevolent spirit. We carried our kayaks past tall Douglas firs, past picnic blankets filled with sunbathing teenagers, hotdog-eating children, and mostly maskless adults. I thought of Kikisoblu and her family, survivors of the Pacific Northwest's previous pandemics. This land has known deadly viruses before.

Over and over, Aram and I paddled up the South Seattle shoreline, around the Sqebeqsed peninsula, watching bald eagles and great blue herons hunt along the shoreline, into the cove that maps label Andrews Bay. Our neighbors started calling it COVID Cove, as people brought their sailboats and motorboats and catamarans from Mercer Island, Gig Harbor, and even farther away, roping them together in flotillas of three or six. They played loud music, tipped back endless beers, danced wildly, and yelled into one another's unmasked faces. We would paddle past the clots of yachts as fast as we could, ignoring occasional jeers at our beat-up kayaks and our masks. Later in the summer, we kayaked past bottles and cans washed up on the Sqebeqsed shoreline, past a homemade white cross planted in honor of a young woman who had fallen off her boyfriend's boat and drowned.

***

Though I live only four blocks from South Seattle's car-clogged arterial, Rainier Avenue, its traffic din doesn't float up the hill to our house. When we first moved here, less than half a mile from where we'd lived for nearly fifteen years, what surprised me most was the birdsong. When we moved to this neighborhood, I realized quickly, after thirty-five years of frequent moves, that I'd finally found my home. I hope to live here for the rest of my life.

Rainier Avenue runs on or very close to an ancient trail that connected Kikisoblu's birthplace, on the shores of Lake Washington, and her deathplace, on Elliott Bay – a place she knew as the Little Crossing Over Place. Very close to my house is a street called Angeline, named in her honor.

I often think of Kikisoblu living in the waterfront cottage that she refused to leave after white settlers decided it was illegal for the Duwamish, Suquamish, and other Native people to live inside Seattle's city limits, to live in their homeplace. Kikisoblu lived in resistance until her death in 1896. Nearly a century later, I began working as a grassroots organizer in Seattle.

***

In early March 2020, when everyone who possibly could began to study, work, shop, and live entirely at home, many of my students saw their lives upended. I was lucky; there are few college subjects easier to teach online than writing. (Which is not to say that it was easy.) By late March, one of my eighteen-year-old students began working full-time as a nursing-home assistant, after one of her parents lost their job. She arrived at our midafternoon Zoom sessions after a full shift at the nursing home, still breathless. She attended via her cell phone, video off to preserve bandwidth, taking notes by hand. Another student attended our Zoom classes sitting on her bunk bed, holding her phone close to her face, microphone off to keep the shouts and screams of three suddenly unschooled children out of our virtual classroom. A third student returned to his village in Alaska and called into class on his cell phone when he wasn't responsible for his younger brother's suicide watch.

Do I need to say that all three are students of color? Meanwhile, some of my white students appeared on Zoom polished and perfectly dressed, their bedrooms stretching enormously and silently behind them.

Two months before our sequestration began, in mid-January, a student had blurted out in the middle of class, "I don't want to die of coronavirus!" I stared at her. What was she talking about? No one in Seattle-Tacoma was going to die of that virus, I had thought.

***

On Leap Day 2020, my goddaughters and I went to the library for the morning and then to a big-box store to buy a Frisbee. It was a blue-sky Saturday, unusually warm for late February. The parking lot was nearly full. I wondered aloud, Why is everyone shopping on a perfect Saturday? Inside, we wound our way around shopping carts piled high, looking for the store's sports section. We ran into a friend, who was buying what looked like six-months' worth of toilet paper. Frisbee in hand, we headed for the long check-out line, passing the shelves that should have held air filters. They were completely empty. A gear clicked in my mind.

We went to Lincoln Park and reveled in the warm grass, graceful breeze, cloudless sky, and shiny new Frisbee floating between us. The park was nearly empty; the day was perfect. Leap Day: a day that rarely happens. It was the last day that I did not worry about the pandemic.

As we drove home, the radio reported a death at a nursing home near Seattle: a man had died of coronavirus the previous evening. Another gear clicked.

***

Three days after Leap Day, after teaching my evening class, I stopped at a twenty-four-hour grocery store on my way home from campus. I filled a large cart: bottles of rubbing alcohol, a large bag of rice, pounds of pasta, latex gloves, multiple bottles of vitamin C and zinc, half a case of wine, and one Virgen de Guadalupe candle.

Two days after that, I took photos of all the bookshelves in my campus office in case I needed someone else to send something to me. I still thought the COVID-19 outbreak would be limited to Seattle and not affect my campus, forty miles away in Tacoma. It did not occur to me that soon there would be no one left on campus to retrieve anything for me.

When I finished taking photos, I stood in the doorway for a long moment. I felt as if I were saying goodbye to the bookshelves, to the gifts from students, to the windows looking out on the square filled with enormous Douglas fir trees. Those trees kept me company as I worked and shaded us when we held class outside. Those trees had shaded the space since the Nisqually, Puyallup, Steilacoom, and Squaxin Island people had cared for this land. Since Kikisoblu had refused to leave her home at the Little Crossing Over Place, had insisted on survival and survivance.

***

On September 12, 2020, the daytime sky is yellow. It doesn't look like night, it looks like some other world. Now our world, I know. I spend the entire day in my bedroom, the only room small enough for an air filter to pull enough soot from the air that it doesn't hurt to breathe. We aren't at risk of evacuation and for that I am grateful. We still have a home. I think of the 1990s, the decade that I devoted to organizing work in favor of an economy that put the needs of people and the planet first. During that decade, so many grassroots movements laid out thirty-year, then twenty-five-year, then twenty-year plans of all that we needed to do (or stop doing) by 2020 to avoid social-ecological collapse. We heeded almost none of those plans.

There is a terribly terrestrial mindset about what we need to do to take care of the planet – as if the ocean somehow doesn't matter or is so big, so vast that it can take care of itself, or that there is nothing that we could possibly do that we could harm the ocean.

~ Sylvia Earle, oceanographer and marine biologist

Growing up in Chicago and then smaller cities and tiny towns in southern Illinois and Indiana, I never imagined I'd someday live on an island in the Salish Sea. Now, after twenty-five years as an islander, I can't picture myself living anywhere but Lopez Island, Washington, one of 419 islands – most of them uninhabited – in the Salish Sea's San Juan Archipelago.

What power draws me to the Salish Sea? It's not just the water's satiny surface on a calm day or the racing white caps when the wind picks up. Part of the attraction is how the color shifts from almost-black to steel gray, to U.S. flag blue, to, occasionally, the blue-green of the Mediterranean. Surely some of the lure is the way the inland water sweeps driftwood to the shore and swirls around bull kelp and sea grasses. Ebbs and floods soothe the soul, even as they pick up velocity and volume with tide changes. I'm always astounded by the majesty of orca whale pods gliding and diving in synchrony; harbor seals' rounded heads, blunt snouts, and brown eyes that pop up at my kayak's stern; and Steller sea lions sunbathing on barnacled rocks.

I attribute my love for the Salish Sea to all these individual features and more. But my true passion is for the way every lovely and fascinating part works with all the others in a latticework of life. Tide pools shelter herring eggs that hatch and feed minke whales. The Salish Sea gifts watershed forests with spawning Pacific salmon such as Chinook, coho, and sockeye – feasts for bears, bald eagles, ravens, and martens. Melting mountain snow glides into rivers that flow into wetlands, empty into bays, and whirl to the sea. The ocean connects to canals and lakes and rivers on other continents, evaporates into clouds, and is filled by rain from skies around the globe.

Over the years, I've learned not just about what I love, but also about the perils that threaten this jewel. If we don't take care of the Salish Sea and all that contributes to it, this interwoven lattice of beauty, wildness, fragility, and relationship will collapse.

As an islander, I spend considerable hours on the Salish Sea, sometimes in a kayak but primarily on the Washington State Ferries (WSF), the largest ferry system in the nation and third largest in the world. The fleet carries nearly twenty-five million people a year through some of the most awe-inspiring scenery on Earth.

While ferries are my connection to the mainland, the Interisland route travels only among the ferry-served islands in the San Juans – Lopez, Shaw, Orcas, and San Juan. Over the years, that circuit has supplied time and space for me to write. In 2018, I became the first-ever writer-in-residence for the Washington State Ferries System, a role I developed and proposed to the agency.

Once or twice a week I walked aboard the *M/V Tillikum* (also known as the Interisland), the vessel that routes passengers around the San Juans. I'd carry my sloshing coffee mug in one hand and wear my backpack filled with books, journals, and my laptop. My "office" measured 310 feet in length, could carry over a thousand passengers and eighty-seven vehicles, and traveled thirteen knots (about fifteen mph) as it cruised. Throughout my one-year term, I usually sat on the passenger deck in a booth with a table and a 360-degree view of the Salish Sea, one of the world's largest inland seas.

Safety regulations require weekly fire drills on the ferry vessels. A crew member announces, "In a few moments, we'll ring alarm bells. This is just a drill, not an actual emergency." I glance at posters in the cabin. They identify passenger gathering stations at each end of the vessel and carry sobering emergency messages. No matter how often I read them I pause, reminded I might need to follow the directions sometime.

> *Emergencies*
> *Go to the nearest Passenger Assembly Station whenever you hear an emergency signal. It is important for your own safety that you follow the directions you are given. Please notify the crew if you have any special training that may be of use during an emergency.*

During this time of climate chaos, many of us create our own assembly stations. Before the COVID-19 pandemic, we gathered in living rooms and around kitchen tables to plan protests, devise strategies to be fossil-fuel free, and write letters to government leaders and corporate executives. When we can't meet face-to-face, we organize virtually. We seek out those with special training and learn from them how to be of use during emergencies such as oil-tanker spills and how they care for sick or dying orcas. Some of us assemble on sacred grounds, in kayaks on the Salish Sea, and at climate conferences. We can no longer deny this is an emergency.

> *Life Jackets*
> *Obtain a life jacket from a designated life jacket locker, underneath a bench seat, or from a crew member. Life jacket locations are clearly marked throughout the vessel. Put on life jackets as instructed by crewmembers. Adults should make sure that children are correctly fitted with their life jackets.*

By ignoring alarms sounded about coal, fracking, endangered owls and orcas and coral reefs, overdevelopment, and overpopulation, we've failed to ensure that our children (and grandchildren) won't need life jackets. Now, thousands of teens like Greta Thunberg of Sweden are instructing us. Their message? "Stop denying, the earth is dying. The seas are rising, and so are we."

> *Abandon Ship*
> *Seven short rings followed by one long ring on the general alarm bells signal abandon ship. Upon hearing the abandon ship signal, go immediately to a Passenger Assembly Station. This order will only be given if the Captain is certain it is safer for you in a life raft than aboard the ferry. When the order to abandon ship is given, the crew will direct you to calmly and quickly move to the designated Embarkation Stations on the car deck. They represent the locations where you would leave the vessel.*

We've been hearing alarm bells for Earth for decades, at least since 1962 when *Silent Spring* author Rachel Carson warned us of the hazards of the pesticide DDT. Now, eyewitness stories, movies about inconvenient truths, and scientific reports make grave predictions about dying rainforests; melting glaciers; rising sea levels; more frequent, catastrophic hurricanes and wildfires; and disappearing species. While I appreciate the ferry crew's weekly drills to prepare for emergencies, the truth is, these climate projections pose much greater threats to our safety.

Earth's oceans, rivers, air, drinking water, forests, and soil constantly sound short and long rings. An Abandon Earth signal, however, is not an option. There are no embarkation stations. There's nowhere a life raft can take us.

We've stayed calm for too long. It's time to move quickly.

This is not just a drill.

TELE AADSEN
CHANGE

The water was warm last summer. Dixon Entrance to Sitka, Southeast Alaska, felt eerily barren – no bait, no birds. All July and August, the coho were skittish, unwilling to school up or settle into traditionally favored spots. With no hot bites to run to, some boats tied up midseason, unable to justify the cost of fuel for the fish they weren't catching. Newer fleetmates trudged the docks looking stunned, confessing they hadn't broken three hundred yet. They'd come in on good years thinking those days were normal. As for Joel and me, Team *Nerka* finally had to practice patience. Notorious runners, always searching for something better – one of our elders once said about Joel, "That boy's jumpier than a fart in a skillet" – we stuck and stayed and tried to make it pay, grinding out days for meager two-digit scores we would've abandoned by midmorning in previous years. When land friends asked how the season was going, we told them the word for the summer was "underwhelming."

Underwhelming. Spoken in true fisherman fashion, understated. Like shrugging "We did all right," when you come back to town with the hold plugged and the waterline sunk. Like green water washing over the windows, coffee cup swan-diving to shards on the floor as your partner in the anchorage asks for a weather report: "It's nautical." Like the calm observation, *the water was warm,* instead of screaming WTF, what's happening, how did we get here?

How did I get here?

Anchorage, 1985. A faded 3x5 captures the moment. A forty-three foot trimaran hovers in the center of the shot, suspended by a crane. My parents, veterinarians in the Mat-Su Valley, have spent the past seven years building the *Askari* in our landlocked backyard. Seven years toiling in the vet clinic every day, laboring deep into every night to achieve this moment, they had reached the long awaited launch. My dad strains at the bow, leather gloves clenched around a guideline. My mom dashes to steady the stern. I am a child supervisor, hands stuffed in pockets, standing on a precipice with the *Askari,* life cleaving into hemispheres of before and after, suspended between land and sea.

That was thirty-five years ago. I'm forty-two now, the same age my mom was when she traded her veterinary license for a troll permit. Imagine – the courage to turn away from your education, the business you'd built, your home, land itself. Sell it all, go all in. Crafting a new reality out of fiberglass, resin, dreams.

Imagine… believing in a dream envisioned, believing in it so profoundly as to sacrifice everything without any guarantees. To sacrifice, suffer even, for the sheer possibility of change.

In December 2019, the news broke that the Gulf of Alaska's cod fishery would be closed for the 2020 season. It was the first fishery to be closed not because of overfishing but as a consequence of warming waters.

A few weeks later, Alaska Fish and Game released their projection for Sitka's sac roe herring fishery, a harvest target of twenty-five thousand tons. Up from 2018's thirteen thousand. The fleet hadn't caught the quota that year, or the year before that. Just finally gave up, charging west to try other regions, other fisheries, leaving disgusted sighs of exhaust in their wake.

I think about herring – a keystone species, their well-being essential to the survival of everyone above them on the food chain, including king salmon – and I think about money, and how fisherfolks are in the VIP seats, front and center as change washes over us, and you know those boats charging west in search of other regions, other fisheries, their engines sound an awful lot like the band on the *Titanic* playing on, playing on, and in my mind they're playing with Tracy Chapman and she's singing *If you knew that you would die today – would you change?*

After the fishing season, I spend winters selling the *Nerka*'s catch. For many of my fleetmates, this is the dream: get your boot in the door with an ice boat, work up to a freezer boat, cut out the middleman and sell your catch yourself. I answer their questions, watch them ascend the industry escalator, their determination to make it, sacrificing, suffering even, for the dream of making a good life catching fewer fish at a greater value.

Meanwhile, over the past five years of slinging salmon to chefs in the surrounding counties, I've driven the equivalent of crossing the country eleven times, often to a soundtrack of NPR, listening to the latest on a melting Arctic & a blazing Australia, thinking about change – climate change, social change, spare change – this show *sucks*, change the channel, burn it all down and start over with systemic change. The ways we're socialized to believe we're supposed to change – moving on up, up, and away, striving for faster, better, more.

Me, I want to slooooooooow down. The more I want is smaller, simpler. More quiet and peace, a care-filled, purposeful present, more acts of kindness and compassion for you and for me, too. This planet is spinning too, too fast and I want off, but how do you stop when your foot is one of billions stuck on the gas pedal? Global change? I might as well be welded to this Chevy Astro, I'm such a part of the machine.

Last September, toward the end of the fishing season, I sat with a fleetmate. His birthday falls in August, smack-dab in what's historically our second king opening. This year, for the first time, he tied the boat up & skipped the opening – a king opening! – to greet his seventy-second year rafting the Alsek River with loved ones instead.

"I never could've imagined doing that," he said. His voice was equal parts awe and gratitude for his decision. I wondered what our world could be like if we all had the security and freedom to make such audacious, life-giving decisions, to measure the value of pounds to dollars to your time's worth, your life's worth. Who among us can afford to do this?

Who can afford not to?

The water was warm last summer. No one denies that. Instead we trade differing takeaways. Some mock a teenage girl's urgent call to action – so direct and fierce, sacrilege to fishing's code of understatement. Others travel to Washington D.C. to lobby to protect the Tongass, the world's largest remaining temperate rainforest. Searching for the magic words to urge people to care, to act, we resort to the language of money. What's it to you?

I do it, too. For every salmon I thank as I slice their gills – *thank you, thank you* – life runs out the scuppers, and by the end of the season I'm running numbers same as anyone else: how many fish at how many pounds at how many dollars to fill how many orders. This is all part of a sea-to-plate story, and I've been living versions of it since I was that seven-year old mariner landing in Sitka, jigging off the dock in Old Thomsen Harbor with fellow boat kids, filling five-gallon buckets with baby black cod. At the end of the day we sold them to my friends' dad for halibut bait. He paid us in ice cream cones from the Dip-n-Sip.

Thirty-five years dragging my hooks through these waters with critical yet marrow-deep devotion. Devotion like being lashed to the mast of a ship cradling you and me and all living things, thrashed by a perfect storm of capitalism, complicity, hypocrisy. When the wind catches its breath, we soothe each other with stories. Stories like when I was twenty-six, crewing for my brother for a king opening, when he pulled a thirty-pounder boat-side. Thick-bellied, not a shimmering scale missing, perfect and perfectly hooked through the tip of her snub nose. He slipped his gaff gently through and popped the hook free. "Go find a river."

That's what keeps me on this ship, you know – faith in those moments when we do the unexpected, do the hard thing, when we go off-script and show what we truly value. When the storm continues but we're not passive. When we reach for the tools before us – science, history, culture, art, community, love – and we make a change.

SARA MALL JOHANI
WILD SALMON WORLD

"Earth's proud orphans lost in a rain green land we've yet to love, now find our desperate joy and simplest wisdom is to follow the seabright salmon home."

This piece was developed for one of the Salmon Festivals which took place annually in Chimacum for several decades. Here's an excerpt from Sara Mall Johani's reflection on the history of the Salmon Festival and Wild Olympic Salmon, which she cofounded with Tom Jay and others in 1987.

Sara Mall Johani
Mine, Yours, Nobody's: Remembering Wild Olympic Salmon 1987–2020

This is the story of a community effort on behalf of Salmon and Nature in Chimacum, Washington. Salmon was our guide, Nature our tutor, the human collective our crucible, the Olympic Peninsula our home. How do people who are all from elsewhere make coherent and lasting community in a "new" place? Maybe the answer is elusive. But in our opinion, the natives of this place should be the deepest guide to our learning to live here. We tried to follow their example. We welcomed the native tribes by inviting them to our annual Salmon Festival. We participated in the historic Paddle to Seattle with the Quileute tribe, joined by the Elwha and other Salish tribes. We hosted the paddlers, providing food and welcome not only for those in the canoe, but also for their support crew and families.

Over several decades, we celebrated our Northwest heritage as Salmon People with a Salmon Festival, as well as interactive education and art projects designed to engage our community: a Trading Card Game, a participatory project called Tracking the Dragon, Noquiklos, the children's climbing sculpture, and a 25-foot long female salmon named FIN, who crisscrossed the country as an interactive display.

Wild Olympic Salmon was eventually designated as part of North Olympic Salmon Coalition, which became focused on restoration and was responsible for restoring several local salmon runs, including Chimacum Creek. Wild Olympic Salmon, now gone, was inspired and spontaneous. It was a spirited and inspiring experiment which may have saved some lives. I was one whose life it saved. Tom [Jay] was another; our participation saved us together. It was our crucible.

Chimacum
April 22, 2020
Earth Day

LEAH SIMEON
THE RIVER ON THE RESERVATION

Ponderosa pine
Sweet summer time
Mornings with coffee
And you
In our camp chairs

Sun and moon balanced on
Two ends of the river
Salmon journeying toward the home
Of the old woman
Who asked Coyote so long ago
To bring them up

CELESTE ADAME
DUWAMISH

Wake I hear quietly. Wake. Wake.
Before light emerges over Rainer,
black walls bleached,
elk drinks
fog lifts.

You whisper into sand
pebbles hit   fluidity of skin.

Whisper names when you slip under surface
emerge chilled
run to fire beyond sands
take from me another bucket
start breakfast for sleeping children
who rise with first rays.

Arroyo has not felt my presence lately
blooming pink flower of prickly pear
cowboy hat at bank
smoke rings dissipate quietly
create yellowed shadows.

excerpt from "Medicine Creek in Four Parts"

SARA MARIE ORTIZ
RIVER

> I could name those birds, see people
> in the clouds. Sight can be polluted
> like a river. When this river asks me:
> where were you when Slavs gave up their names
> to find good homes on paved streets west of here?
> I talk back. What are you, river?
> Only water, taking any bed you find.
> All you have is current, doubled back
> on in-tide, screaming out on out.
> I am on your bank, blinded and alive.

from *Duwamish Head* by Richard F. Hugo

Name those birds.
See people.
In the clouds.
> *little errant bits of song*

What
is
the
river?

What *are* you, river?

What is it to be in relationship with river like a poem, river like a child, river like a deep breath? It is a spirit reckoning. And it is one of which we are all a part whether we see it and name it or not.

What do you know, people of the inside?

COVID really hit in March of 2020, or the reality of it in the Seattle area really hit at that time, and I have since wondered a lot about connection to house, to home, to place, to river. I knew I'd be spending more time contemplating my relationship to house and to river and to my own heart than I would with people. So I settled in. Always a turning. Always an itinerant start and stare – looking awkwardly in. I am an awkward poet. And I don't mind that.

I love White Center. I didn't always. I used to have very judgy feelings toward the neighborhood. I moved to Seattle from my desert home, and *my river,* the Rio Grande, years ago now; moved from my beloved home deep in the arid northern desert of Santa Fe, New Mexico, and Albuquerque where a child me grew to be a woman. When I first came to the city for work and for love I had no fucking idea. I had no idea about the lives of the people who lived, and dreamed, and loved and worked here. I would end up spending lots of time serving and working in the neighborhood known as White Center and would learn more and more about the fears and dreams of the many families, children, youth, elders, workers, students, artists – all in the area south of Seattle and lining the ancestral riverways and Salish Sea. I've listened and absorbed so many biases, so many stereotypes and perceptions about the city of Seattle and the many communities that are both being squeezed out and kept out. I'm glad to call the south end my home.

Sight can be polluted like a river.

All of my work in community, particularly serving the American Indian and Alaska Native community, is guided by both precept and a preternatural instinct to at once interrogate and honor origins. Every story is a birth story. Every story – even those about death (sometimes especially these) – are about birth and the cyclic nature of all things. This is what I've been taught. Never in all of my journeying, and wondering, and writing have I ever stood in the garden of this like this. Not in quite this way. The pandemic is teaching us all things.

Particularly the lessons we must keep learning and learning.

The story of The Changer (Dukʷibəɬ) contains the lessons of this world and the next.

The pandemic is teaching us about relationship with place. The pandemic is teaching us about our relationship with story. The pandemic is teaching us about the importance of our relationships with memory and with each other. Like Hugo's meditation on sight being polluted like the river, so too is memory and our connection to other people and all the living things of the universe. Some things that are polluted cannot be reversed or repaired. But there is still hope.

My big fluffy orange mountain kitty who arrived one night in early winter and who we call Mr. Pickles is getting me through this thing.

These are uncertain times. I am struggling – as most are – to keep working, keep hoping, and I am struggling, I find, to prioritize things artfully and accordingly. I meditate a lot on my relationship to all things pre-pandemic and what living in this beautiful and sometimes beastly place south of Seattle – the land and neighborhoods of the area called Highline, threaded through by the Duwamish River, the Sound, and all the many buildings and man-made elements on the land and water – means, these streets that sing a song of "take" and "remake at all costs," to me.

School buildings figure prominently in this cartography for me because I am a teacher. And a teacher of teachers. The pandemic has changed and deepened my perception of teaching and what it means to be a teacher. My beloved grandmother Foster was a schoolteacher in a small southern desert town. She gave her life and love to her work. She was one of my first and most important teachers. And I know as I shift from Zoom 1,047 to Zoom god-even-knows-how-many that her teachings *about* teaching live in me. It's never been more important that I retrace their steps. Though she taught in a very different time, the 1950s through the 1990s, I know those traced lines are guiding me. I never wanted to be a teacher and never thought I'd encourage others to teach either. But the process of being in education, and of teaching, has taught me more about writing, about giving and receiving, about opening one's self to the world, in a way that writing alone could not have.

Never underestimate the river.

I once wrote a poem. It was called "Letter to You, Child of the Next World."
It was a contained rage.
A contained hopeful thing.
A sadness both rising up and the silt of it flowing and dropping back down as the river needs.
It was a river, this poem.
I've since written it and rewritten it in differing light.
Perhaps every poem I write is the same poem; a poem to you, child of the next world.
I hope you have some hope.
I hope you take into the cup of your hands the food and medicine of this time, pandemic and all, and all the ancestral lines back. Take it up into your hands.

And discard what you can't use.
I wish I had more wisdom for you.

Much of what I have to offer is in the saying at all and not staying silent every time.
What little I know is here.
The river can be an only and every god for those who know.
If you spend enough time with the river it will teach you most (not all, this is important) of its secrets.

Know, child of the next world,
that a river can be a ghost. And that ghosts can be rivers too.
Know, children of the next world, that this truth is telling and singing
in the hearts of its women as well.

Know too, child, that everyone's apocalypse is different.

JENIFER BROWNE LAWRENCE
LANDSCAPE WITH NO NET LOSS

This is the river's fingertip, pink bulb-end of a wild onion.
The sun leaps from the water and drops into the forest.
Bits of blown deer lichen float off without license.
I have changed a fuse in the dark. Have shoveled
trenches for cable, pulled the sway-end of a survey chain
until my palms blistered. I flirt with mosquitos in gray light,
wish I still smoked, stub my boot toes at the marsh edge.
From the estuary, up comes the mist in faltering heat.
Longfin smelt change direction midair, belly-slap
to avoid the Chinook or shake loose eggs
or just for the hell of it, who knows, we are all
bouncing off one body and into another.
On the map, or from the treetops, the river mouth
is a hand spread wide to catch everything.

LAUREN SILVER
MORE THAN WE CAN BEAR

It's been a week since the attack on the US Capitol, and here on the edge of the salty Salish
Sea, dark, dense clouds cracked open and dumped torrential rains. Not our usual gentle
drip, drip, dripping rain; no, this was two days and two nights of raging rainfall, following a
similar drenching the week before – leaving the ground completely saturated. She, the
ground beneath our feet and the plants and trees who dwell in her midst, had done their
best to absorb the great waters that tore out of our skies.

There was just   too   much   water.

On the third morning, the storm finally moved on. The wooly blanket of clouds began to
thin;
charcoal sky gradually shifted to a brilliant blue. Sunshine embraced us with arms wide
open. After deep, grief-filled heartbreak, we were blessed with a sunny day – in January.

I tell you, that is a miracle in these parts.

In the midst of a sunlit afternoon, driving along a road I travel often, I saw something that
grabbed at my grieving heart. It was not a creek or a stream, not a river. No. This was a
simple drainage ditch who'd gone from her usual trickle to a slow, lazy meander, to a raging
force leaping up and out of her muddy banks – a fierce and sparkling water dragon roiled
and
thrashed, then folded in upon herself, before tumbling out to the sea.

When I saw that crazy-out-of-her-mind drainage ditch
I knew I'd be all right. I knew we
would be all right.

these mighty waters knew what to do
in this time of
more than we can bear
we must
overflow.
Somehow, we will find our way
we, with our broken-wide-open hearts
we will become that churning drainage ditch that flows and flows and flows
and finally makes her way to the great, salty Mother Waters
who generously
receives all our tears

She can receive all of us; every bit
all the waters that have crashed down upon us
and in time, in a Great-Mother-Waters kind of time
we will find our way.

PRISCILLA LONG
DURING THE PANDEMIC

This is happening right here, right now,
on this cold sleet day in February,
a fire in the fireplace puts yellow-orange
into bleak gray tones. Across the room
the zebra plant, exiled from Brazil,
looks content, even vivid after I water
its roots and dark green leaves.
This is happening right here, right now,
the people across the street turn on
Christmas lights every night to speak
for Peace on Earth, and next door
the two lawyers and their two girls
read books together and make Christmas
cookies in February. This is happening,
I swear, right now, poetry readings,
cello concerts on Zoom every evening.
All over town people are writing
letters again, working on their rusty
handwriting, purchasing cream-colored
stationery. Oh, and photography
is flourishing, spectacular sunsets
shot by Dharmamitra, my good
friend. The raccoons, raucous rascals,
are pleased with lack of traffic. The poets
are composing, the painters are painting,
the children are having pillow fights
and the lovers, too, pitch pillows
at each other between kisses. The yoginis,
meanwhile, have perfected downward-facing
dog. The dogs could not be more pleased,
their masters ever-home. Yes, there is sickness,
cruelty also, chronic crying, grief, anxiety,
and yes, the rent is due. But, happening right here,
right now, the hellebores are blooming purple,
the osoberry can hardly wait for spring.

MARIE EATON
A DREAM PLANTING ITSELF, MAY 27, 2020

In the midst of this terrible despair, can we rethink the doomsday machine we have built for ourselves?

~ Arundhati Roy, "The Pandemic Is a Portal," *Financial Times*, April 3, 2020.

Skies clear over Delhi
and Mt. Everest can be seen from northern India
for the first time in recorded history.

A family of Egyptian geese cross
the empty tarmac of Tel Aviv's Ben Gurion Airport.
Flocks of wild turkeys strut around Harvard Yard
as if they remember forests that once grew there.

Perhaps this enforced isolation gifts us
with the silence we need
to listen
to alarm bells of climate breakdown,
raging forest fires, rapid Arctic ice melt,
species extinction.

Perhaps we have been given
visions of recovery, renewal,
and resurgence.

Images of antlers
glimpsed through shadowy power lines,
turtles and seabirds on wide, deserted sands,
dolphins in Venice canals,
and the sweet wild chorus of morning birds
are more than flesh and feather and bone.

Emissaries of hope and possibility,
they are a dream planting itself,
daring us to imagine a better world.

"A dream planting itself" is a line from the poem "For Calling the Spirit Back from Wandering the Earth in Its Human Feet" by Joy Harjo, from Conflict Resolution for Holy Beings *(W. W. Norton, 2015).*

BARBARA DRAKE
TULIPS AND GARLIC

Fall 2020

Today I am planting tulips and garlic – the bulbs
one at a time go into the earth, each in its little grave.

This is important business, and my mood is grave.
As days grow colder and darker, I imagine spring

and the joy of tulips and garlic, how they will spring
up gaily from the warming ground.

But today I bury them deep in the ground.
It's so dark in the earth, and I feel a little afraid

as they go under – there are reasons to be afraid.
No matter – little bulbs I will see you in spring. I promise

we will have festive reunions. Or more than a promise –
I take a sacred vow, cast a magic spell in soil, I will greet you.

Imagine a spring without tulips and garlic. Can you?
In the dark days of autumn, we must not neglect planting bulbs.

KELLI RUSSELL AGODON
IN PRAISE OF OYSTERS

for the Yamashita family

In praise of oysters, of a family
replanting the tidelands, in praise
of strength, *It gives me great pleasure*
　　to be able to share of what we have,
in praise of boats, wooden boxes
of seeds, straw and rice mats.
　　He imported pearls from Japan at one time,
cities built from shells, *mother-of, father-of*
community, in praise of staying,
in replenishing what was overharvested,
what pollution stole.
　　　　There's nothing better
than oysters – I hear echoes
in the shoreline. How to live optimistically
in a country of internment camps, a grandfather
sent to Montana, a family forced to California,
　　it was challenging, but at the same time,
　　there were very kind people. Praise Masahide
and the renamed Pacific oyster, to be a gem
in a nation of rough tides – praise
the family and the thousands of seeds
to shellfish farmers, to make the shorelines glisten,
to always share what we have.

PENINA TAESALI
THE WORD OF THE DAY

Every Day Is Earth Day

The word of the day could be *dreadful* or *atrocious* or *lost,* for the roses root deeper for cleaner water to survive this August. Their petals pealing to blossom, our eyes open so we may protect the wild green dawn   so we could stop.   let the unexpected tributaries off 14th Street & Madras stream for the mallard and her drake with the seven ducklings paddling through the narrow brook of the First Peoples lands mourning for Mother Earth

and the word of the day tomorrow? Let it not be brutality or money or rifle or my religion or yours   let it be leopard or rhinoceros or red abalone or blue whale or Yangtze River dolphin or let the word be African talking drum or Fijian canoe drum or Pilipino kulingtang or Appalachian dulcimer or ukulele or slack-key guitar or let it be trombone carried on the confident shoulders of a ten-year-old girl — let us think the where and how and why

we pick up and play and write and sing and dance so that the Honduran emerald hummingbird the leatherback sea turtle the mountain gorilla the tiger salamander the fender blue butterfly the honeybees the living coral reefs the breathing rainforests in Brazil in Guinea and here in the Sacramento Delta where river otters fish and breed   let our word be bigger as in humility as in mountain water tree food sun moon stars for them for them for them

ANITA LEIGH HOLLADAY
RESILIENCE

When I was growing up, my parents would often describe my breathlessly ecstatic reaction upon first seeing big trees, redwoods, as a toddler on vacation. Most of my adult life I've chosen to live under redwoods or within walking distances to cedar-filled forests. I've always loved the implicit metaphor of nurse logs; I'm now learning more about how they function in a forest, training my eye to see where trees have grown large but still bear traces of their beginnings, growing on and over and being nourished – still – by a fallen tree as it slowly, slowly becomes soil. Though I photograph many aspects of nature, some of my favorite beings to document are old trees.

Nancy Lord
On the Good Land

As we battled our way through the 2020 pandemic, most of us discovered a few new things to be grateful for. One of these for me has been taking the time to explore the trails and open spaces in and around my home place – Homer, Alaska, on the shores of Kachemak Bay. While I've always enjoyed walking and hiking with friends, what's new to me is the social distancing of so much wandering on my own, moving slowly and attentively over the land.

In June, when I paused by the meadow along the Calvin-Coyle Trail, on a property deeded to and managed by our local land trust, I inhaled the scent of pushki (cow parsnip) plants warmed by the sun and could not help thinking, *Take time to smell the roses.* So often in the demands of our pre-pandemic lives, we didn't do that. We were busy people. We're still busy, but there's been room in this last year – for some of us – to force a pause, to stick near home, to align what we do with what might bring us the needed stillness to think about where we are, *why* we are, what responsibilities we hold not just to one another but to the more-than-human world.

In my solitary walks, with no distracting talk, no adjustments to another's timetable or desires, I've rediscovered field and forest routes all through and around my town, with groves of birch trees, babbling brooks, the song of a Pacific wren and the stare of a young hare. Small things, easily overlooked as we rush through life without the patience or the calm to stop and observe, and to reflect.

Still early in the pandemic, I found the songbirds quieting from the symphony of earlier weeks. They no longer needed to impress one another. I stopped at a rustling in the dead leaves beneath alders, taking in an anxious cheeping, then recognizing the blazing cap of a golden-crowned sparrow. It was being chased through the underbrush by a fledgling so puffed out it was nearly twice its size. For long minutes, I watched the parent bird dipping and diving in the duff, pulling up bugs to feed into the young one's demanding open mouth.

Elsewhere I paused to admire the bright purple nagoonberry flowers, the delicate trailing raspberry blooms, the dwarf dogwoods. The broad devil's club leaves, some already reaching over my head, filtered the light and spread it over forests of ferns.

As I returned to the same trail in later weeks, I watched it all unfold – prickly stalks shooting up, tight fiddleheads unfurling, warblers darting through treetops. Everything was growing, changing, every day, every minute, even as I watched and listened. I was reminded of Heraclitus's words: "No man ever steps in the same river twice, for it's not the same river and he's not the same man." Another day it wasn't sparrows stopping me, it was snipes flying, a rotted snag falling apart, a new moose calf. In another week, two weeks, a month, I was among fireweed in bloom, flowers turned to berries, the wetland yellowing; I was feeling a cold wind. By year's end, the world was quieter still, snow softly falling, ice filigreeing over the creek. The dry pushki umbrels wore crowns of frost, and the ground-hugging wintergreen stayed true to its name. I followed the tracks of moose, hare, squirrel, shrew. I listened to the wingbeats of silent crows.

I thought often of those who came before me, who found sustenance in this land and cared for it. This is Dena'ina land, the southern edge of homeland for Athabaskan people who long ago left inland forests to live on the shores of a generous bay. This whole peninsula they called Yaghanen, the Good Land. They knew the animals and plants – the golden-crowned sparrow singing its three-syllable name, tsik'ezdlagh, and the devil's club, heshkeghka'a, literally "prickle-big-big." They had a word for the spring snow that melts the snow beneath it, a word that translates to "one that eats snow."

More recently, the settlers, the homesteaders, arrived to claim the land as their own, to cut trees and build cabins, grow hay, keep cattle and chickens. It was a hard land for them, and many turned to the sea for food and livelihood. The homesteads divided and redivided, and some portions were saved, conserved now for wildlife and open space. Some public lands, too – important habitats for moose, baby salmon, migrating shorebirds – were protected by public wish and demand.

A gift of the pandemic year to me, then, has been this: awareness and appreciation. I've learned to more deeply value the place where I live and what it can teach me. And I'm grateful for those who came before me, who have cared for the land that cares for us in ways we seldom take the time to acknowledge. Our history, which can seem so short in this part of the world, reveals itself from every turn in the trail, every track, every newfound thought. Whatever comes next, the lands that sustain us – always changing, always renewing, tender with their many lives – will be essential to carrying on.

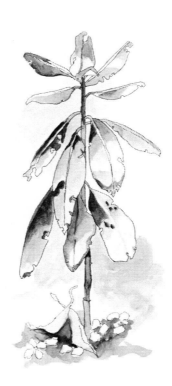

CAROLYN SERVID
YOU SAY THIS IS YOUR LAND. WHERE ARE YOUR STORIES?

for Dorik Mechau

> The Tlingit elder travels to the meeting to present his people's deed, as recorded on a ceremonial blanket of his Sockeye Salmon Clan. The blanket has been passed from generation to generation in an unbroken line, this history of the land and its people woven into mountain goat wool, from a time before the Puritans' first Thanksgiving. His granddaughter holds the blanket for him, translating his Tlingit words. Her grandfather tells how the Tlingit land was formed, how Raven made the waters, how the trees and plants came to be, how the people realized their kinship with the sockeye salmon, how the rules governing the use of land and waters came of the need to protect that kinship. Her grandfather shows how the Tlingit people and their land and its resources continued as one for thousands of years, continues to this day. Her grandfather says, "You say this is your land. Where are your stories?"[1]

The elder was Austin Hammond, the distinguished and deeply admired traditional leader of the Lukaax̱.ádi Tlingit clan whose people had a unique historical relationship with Sockeye Point on Chilkoot Lake, north of the town of Haines, Alaska. The lake receives the water of the glacier-fed Chilkoot River, which flows through a rugged, commanding, ice-ridden spread of mountains that squeeze the northern end of Lynn Canal and the reaching fingers of its various inlets. It is a powerful, richly inhabited landscape. The stories Austin Hammond knew from the centuries-old Tlingit oral tradition are about that place and its inhabitants – people and salmon, people and brown bear, people and killer whale, people and glaciers and tides and mountains and trees, people who go under the blanket of the sea to visit distant relatives. Like the stories of any literature, they profile human character through accounts of pride, greed, envy, alienation, allegiance, honor, and love. But a fundamental characteristic of these Tlingit stories is that they tell of human lives inextricably intertwined with the land. They describe primary relationships of kinship and reciprocity, of obligation and appropriate behavior, between people and the web of living things that nurtures and sustains them.

Like any oral storytelling tradition, the Tlingit oral tradition allows the chance for a given story to be told and heard again and again. There is reason for the repetition. People take from stories what they are ready for, what their life experiences allow them to understand. The power of stories is that they have depth and dimension that allow for multiple levels of meaning. They outlast us. They wait for us to comprehend their significance. As Barry Lopez noted in *Crow and Weasel*, "Sometimes a person needs a story more than food to stay alive. That is why we put these stories in each other's memory. This is how people care for themselves."[2]

With his rich oral tradition of Tlingit stories, Austin Hammond has an advantage over most of us – a rootedness in place that goes back as far as the collective Tlingit memory. The stories both describe and *pre*scribe a set of human values toward the land. Inherent in these stories and values is a reality becoming more cogent for us all at this moment in human history, one that simply has to do with survival.

It strikes me that Austin Hammond's knowledge and relationship to his homeland are deeply infused with intimacy. As his question implies, if we claim ownership to land, we need to know it deeply, so deeply that it infuses our very being and our culture through our stories. For Austin Hammond, the sense of belonging inherent in ownership of the land goes two ways – the land belonged to his people, but the people also belonged to the land, on the land, in that particular place. Intimacy is something we easily assign to relationships between human beings. But in the Western tradition, it is far less common for us to think about intimate human relationships with the land. Science explores the complexity of the natural world in precise and intricately detailed ways that might suggest an intimate kind of knowing, but scientific protocol requires that the accumulated body of scientific knowledge rest on a foundation of objectivity. Austin Hammond's intimate knowledge, while rooted in centuries of observation, is also rooted in centuries of reciprocal engagement, of cultural traditions and stories that provide space for the human heart to acknowledge the indebtedness of human beings to all that the land provides for their survival.

Most of us don't have such stories ready at hand. Most of us don't have long-established intimate relationships to the land we inhabit, the places we live. And the deed we have to whatever piece of land or property we might own is a flat, thin piece of paper with virtually no dimension, covered with text written in legal language that tells no story. It describes the land as a blank slate, objectively defining it by its size and precisely where it is located in a particular community, city, county, or borough as delineated by specific north, south, east, and west degrees of longitude and latitude. Our deeds strip the land of any sense of life. They say nothing of the relationship between people and the land. They simply acknowledge ownership of property within designated boundaries based on a monetary payment for the land. They may be signals of wealth but not of the well-being of the land and its owner.

Austin Hammond's deed, the sacred ceremonial Chilkat blanket, was made to be worn by a respected leader of his community, of his Tlingit clan. It was made to dance in, to come alive with the history of ancestors and their descendants depicted in the figures intricately woven into the blanket. It was brought into being by a skilled woman's hands, one of his own people, created out of the very warp and weft of his culture, made with mountain goat wool and yellow cedar bark from the place his people have inhabited for thousands of years. Austin Hammond's deed has been integral, essential, to his people's survival.

One of the most powerful tools we have for seeing our way through this moment in history – through the crises of climate change, politics, economy, social justice, and pandemic – is the human imagination. "Sometimes a person needs a story more than food to stay alive," says Barry Lopez. While we cannot simply appropriate the stories of another culture to fix the confused and failing systems that are the underpinnings of our own, we *can* imagine into being the stories we need. We can root ourselves, ground ourselves, in the places we live. We can pay specific attention, community by community, neighborhood by neighborhood, to where we are and who is congregated there with us – fellow human beings of all persuasions; fellow mountains, rivers, plants, and trees; fellow animals, birds, insects – taking stock of all that is integral to the local ecosystem and what is essential for that whole ecosystem's well-being. We can hold up those home-ground stories to the light to educate ourselves, to challenge and inspire us, to find common purpose, to collaborate in the interest of the whole. We can seek out the wisdom of durable traditions to guide us. We can ask and ask the question "What if?" and pool our collective, most creative energies to imagine stories with constructive, grounded answers.

The storyteller's art is rooted in resilience, in understanding the capacity of the human heart and mind to face challenges and obstacles, to imagine and craft and finesse ways to overcome them. The seed for those stories lives in possibility, the narrow crack of a window that exists in the darkness of uncertainty. A narrow crack that can open to the question "What if?" The question that provides light for the new stories we need to come into being.

———————————

1. "Of Two Minds" by Mary Kancewick in *From the Island's Edge: A Sitka Reader* edited by Carolyn Servid (Graywolf Press, 1995).

2. *Crow and Weasel* by Barry Lopez (North Point Press, 1990).

A few resources among many:

If This Is Your Land, Where Are Your Stories? Finding Common Ground by J. Edward Chamberlin (Knopf Canada, 2003).

From What Is to What If? Unleashing the Power of the Imagination to Create the Future We Want by Rob Hopkins (Chelsea Green Publishing, 2019).

The Way of the Imagination: Essays by Scott Russell Sanders (Counterpoint, 2020).

Braiding Sweetgrass: Indigenous Wisdom, Scientific Knowledge, and the Teachings of Plants by Robin Wall Kimmerer (Milkweed Editions, 2013).

Moral Ground: Ethical Action for a Planet in Peril, edited by Kathleen Dean Moore and Michael P. Nelson (Trinity University Press, 2010).

The Community Resilience Reader: Essential Resources for an Era of Upheaval, edited by Daniel Lerch (Island Press, 2017).

Resilience.org, a website of the Post Carbon Institute, Corvallis, Oregon

KATHLEEN ALCALÁ
ANCESTORS AND STRANGERS

Every day I wake up thankful that I live in the Northwest. I grumble about the cold, the wet, the darkness, but as I drink coffee and peer outside, I can see the madronas and Douglas firs waiting for me. Around the corner is the big-leaf maple, stalwart, usually silent, but expressing her opinions clearly.

There are many stories I could tell about my relationship with trees. Some I have shared on my blog and at least one in the local newspaper, but mostly I have kept them to myself. This is private, my relationship with trees. It is my refuge when people get to be too much for me.

As the pandemic quarantine has drawn out over more and more time, I have come to realize that I probably could not have survived this in a big city. Friends described staying indoors for weeks and weeks during the worst of it, when their dear friends and older family members died as much for lack of treatment as for the severity of the disease.

I suggested to a friend in Massachusetts that he take his children hiking as a way to get outside, but he said the trails were too narrow to keep a distance from other hikers, as well as crammed with others desperate to get out.

As a college student, I began working summers in Washington, D.C. I could make more there than in my hometown of San Bernardino, California, even factoring in transportation to the East Coast, food, and rent. But as I took my lunchbreaks outdoors just to see the sky, sometimes skipping lunch to walk around the block, it became clear to me that I would never survive a 9 to 5 job in a room where I could not see outside. And a sign of status in that town is to have a window. I would not live long enough, I realized, to ever earn a window.

My house here in the Northwest has floor-to-ceiling windows on the south side, welcoming in whatever sunlight is available. I can walk in a marsh (well, on a boardwalk), I can walk on a trail along the highway (a trail I fought against when I learned how many trees would be destroyed), and I can walk into what passes for town. One summer, my husband showed me some of the trails left over from when people walked everywhere on this island, transportation being limited to canoes and horses. The teenagers in Eagledale rowed boats across Eagle Harbor to attend high school because there was no direct overland route.

I kept saying, "Are we supposed to be here?" as we cut across backyards and scooted up and down walls and cement stairs between properties. We walked to the unpaved end of a road where, if you crouch down and look across the land, you can see the even furrows where strawberries were once grown by the Koura family for export. There are small shacks that once sheltered First Nations berry pickers, some of whom came all the way from Canada for the work. There is something both disturbing and calming about these places, lost in time but still here, like a forgotten shirt at the back of the closet. They speak to us from a time when people lived by the seasons and getting the strawberries in from the fields and to market meant the success or failure of many people on the island. The berry pickers intermarried with the Filipino population to create an ethnic group unique to the island; they call themselves Indipinos.

I am aware that my sense of history, of nature, and of who I am as a person is completely intertwined with the landscape of the West. Once I thought that I was flexible enough to live anywhere, anywhere, but quarantine has shown me otherwise. There are other places that I have called home, and places that I have visited often for their beauty and tranquility. But the small-town West is where I can unwind enough to turn my attention to creating something new.

The feeling is that nature is taking care of things, things that I would need to take care of otherwise. I know that sounds crazy, and clearly there are times when nature could use a helping hand. I have volunteered to weed parks and pick up trash. But I am the sort of person who, when I try these things, someone comes along and says, "Here, I'll take that," and gently guides me out of the zone of engagement. I've come to realize that my writing – about my family in nineteenth- century Mexico, my indigenous ancestors in the Sonoran Desert, and speculative fiction about what our future on a badly kept planet might look like – is the most powerful support I can offer. My book *The Deepest Roots: Finding Food and Community on a Pacific Northwest Island* describes the many interlocking systems that support our local food supply, from plant starts to the grocery store. While we come from a variety of backgrounds and personal philosophies, most islanders would agree that it is a privilege to live here, but it takes a delicate balance to maintain these systems.

While I love to go hiking, I am always glad to come home to a warm, dry house. I keep a vegetable garden that gives me great pleasure, both in keeping it and eating from it. The plants unfold in all good time and yield themselves up for consumption. There are plants and animals, such as chickens and clams, that thrive when cultivated by humans, affirming that line between humans and nature as a place of beauty, creativity, and sustenance. There are also wild mushrooms, their locations fiercely guarded by those "in the know." I am not one of them, but I am happy to eat the mushrooms if offered.

White settlers saw the West as an untamed wilderness, but all across the country Indigenous people had already bred and crafted countless fruit orchards, cornfields, squash, and beanfields. Books such as *Another America: Native American Maps & the History of Our Land,* by Mark Warhus, open our eyes to a carefully attended landscape that nevertheless remained undivided by barbed wire or other barriers to the seasonal flow of herd migration, seasonal fish passage, or migrating flocks of birds.

In the Northwest, the Puget Sound tribes carefully cultivated clam beds that led to even more clams and grew camas roots that could be dried and pounded together with salmon to create portable, nutritious cakes. Besides the productive ocean, the Pacific Northwest forests offered a wide array of edible plants. Villages and settlements were inhabited seasonally, so people moved from campsite to campsite as food became available rather than taking all the time and expense to ship food across the country to stationary dwelling places as we do now. Imagine a time before plastic clogged our shorelines and the burning of oil had destabilized the weather. Imagine when not one thing had been manufactured that would not break down to its basic, nontoxic elements.

What the forest and its cultivated edges say to me is: Listen. Pay attention. We are here for you, but you must not take us for granted. Do not waste this time or place. We love you and want you to write wild stories about ancestors and strangers. Meanwhile, we – the trees, the wild roses, salal, and mushrooms – will continue to tell one another stories that you don't understand. Yes, you can walk among us and listen to the wind in the treetops, but here, let me take that from you. Have a cup of rosehip tea and weave your own stories.

Until I visited Moxee on a balmy summer afternoon, I had never seen a field of growing hops. The day I first stumbled on one, I was making my way back to Seattle from a trip to the Maryhill Museum of Art and the Columbia River Gorge. After I had driven more than an hour, the road narrowed and in front of me were hundreds of slender, verdant vines stretching to the heavens. Jack of the beanstalk would have been pleased with the climbing opportunities and the geometry of the long poles and wire lines that kept the vines upright.

I returned to the area that November to visit schools in the small town of Mattawa, which sits on a hillock surrounded by apple orchards and grape vines. Since Mattawa did not have accommodations, I decided to spend the night in Yakima, knowing that to reach the schools I would have to drive through Moxee and the hop fields. I took the wheel at 6:30 a.m. to make the hour-plus drive and arrive at the middle school on time. It was a cold day, not my forte, but I was encouraged by the delight ahead: tall celadon stalks swaying in tender morning light. But all I found were barren fields reeking with the pungent smell of macerated bovine waste. The harvested hops were probably long on their way to becoming beer.

To my good fortune, the drive from Moxee to Mattawa is stunning with or without burgeoning hops. At that early hour I shared the road with the occasional sedan, more often with trucks, and now and then with a hawk sweeping over the golden, grassy expanse looking to snatch up breakfast. The Columbia River runs to the west and is not visible from the two-lane road, but its water, brought over a significant distance and over very steep terrain, is what makes the hops, apples, and pears that grow in the otherwise arid landscape around Moxee possible.

Fifty minutes from Yakima the road goes no farther. It ends in front of an entrance to the Hanford Nuclear Site. The gate brought to an abrupt end my early-morning reverie through the bucolic landscape awash in buttery light. It is a stark moment, to face the gate. Nuclear weapons were constructed and tested over this very landscape, and the site, next to the river, still contains vats of contaminated nuclear material.

The choice at the gate is thus: turn right and head to Richland or turn left and descend the steep bluff to the Vernita Bridge, which crosses the Columbia River a few miles south of the Priest Rapids Dam. I turned left, and suddenly found myself immersed in an entirely different weather system. Where there had been sunshine, now the thickest fog imaginable made it hard to distinguish land from sky. The river too had birthed a twin sister of evaporated water, which turned and curled thickly directly above itself. I worked hard to hug the right edge of the road. The big rigs passing me in the opposite direction could, like me, see exactly nothing in front of them.

Once I crossed the bridge, I knew that soon to my right grew extensive apple orchards. I knew that to my left basalt cliffs and a native sagebrush steppe witnessed the river's current. I knew that soon, on my left, the turnoff for the Wanapum Heritage Center would appear. The Wanapum did not sign a treaty and have been able to remain, to this day, close to their ancestral village on the Columbia plateau.

The wind can be very powerful in these parts. When I drove through back in August, I tried a detour to visit the riverbank, but the poplar barriers that protect the orchards swirled, heaved, and twisted violently. I feared branches from mature trees would snap off and land on my car, or worse, on me. I abandoned my quest and drove home instead. But after a day at the schools, buzzing with students' energy, I made my way to a nature park outside the town of Desert Aire to stand at the river's edge.

Taking in the riparian scenery I considered my interactions with the students. Almost all of them are the sons and daughters of the men and women who tend to the grapes, cherries, hops, and apples that grow here with such profusion. After a poetry workshop at the high school, I invited students to share their compositions. Some students preferred speaking of what they had written. One girl talked about swimming in the river's inky waters on a late summer night.

A young man shared how the past summer he, his sister, and his parents went on a river outing. He told how it was late evening when they waded into the river. He described how the light reflected off the water and illuminated his smiling mother's face. He shared how rarely they were together as a family and how more rare it was to be together enjoying a moment of leisure. He told us that both his parents worked the fields, which means long, long hours of physically grueling work. As he spoke, the light, the water, his mother, his father, the joy of the afternoon, the love for his family flushed over his lovely young face. The beauty of the moment he described touched us all.

With birdcalls around me, with the wind's gentle susurrations through the treetops, I thought of the young man and his family. I thought of the Wanapum. I thought of my travels along the Columbia, of the gorgeous plateau where Moxee is located, of deep lavender and blazing orange sunsets, of what it means to love a place. For the Wanapum there is no other. Generations of living over these steppes and plateaus, of watching light sometimes deepen, sometimes flatten surfaces, the river birthing its twin. This terrain could not be without them as they and the land are one.

We learn to love the place in which we are born because we develop relationships to other people, to the vegetation, to animals, and to the terrain itself. Rocks and cliffs, sandy banks, sheer walls, drifting clouds, seep into our bones and into language. The language of a place is also part of its ecosystem. Languages carry the specificity of a particular terrain. This is why peoples who live near the Artic have multiple names for snow, and Native peoples who've lived for millennia along the Columbia River call salmon by different names depending on the season. And this is how for a native of El Salvador like me, a mango is never just a mango but qualified according to its evolution toward perfect ripeness.

Terrain and language dwell inside us. So, how is it that people born elsewhere, who carry inside themselves other landscapes, other speech sounds, come to love a new place? How are those who are made of corn, say, come to feel they are made of cottonwood? The question, and its answer, may seem silly or obvious, but it is worth considering, especially in the socially fragmented, environmentally precarious world we live in now. An openness of spirit is part of it, a willingness to see and understand what resonances give the new terrain its coherent geography, and to observe within ourselves how the new place may share resonances with the old we carry within. Humans are omnivores of landscape. We can successfully adapt to a new place, even if sometimes it feels a bit too cold or too hot. Human intelligence and capacity make it possible for us to learn a new language and to accommodate ourselves to new surroundings.

Carl Sauer, a geographer writing in the 1930s, defined geography as an organic unit that comprehends land and life in terms of each other. A place is terrain and the cultural formations that happen within its boundary. In other words, living forms are inseparable from spatial relationships, and these relationships flourish between humans, between species of the natural world, and between humans and nature. Place is the physical manifestation of an environment and the web of relations that thrive upon it.

There are, of course, individual temperaments and preferences that make someone seek and attach themselves to a new place even if vastly different from the one inherited. But for most of us, we learn to love a place by living in it. Loving a place means depositing enough layers of experience in one place so that it becomes pivotal to our daily life. The longer we interact with a place, its nuances and hues reveal themselves. But in order to make memories that will attach us to a given place we humans need connections based on mutual respect and love.

Loving something means taking care of it, valuing it, ensuring its maintenance and well-being.

Chief Se'alth of the Suquamish and Duwamish tribes said that we are part of a carefully calibrated web of life and that when we diminish one part of it, we alter the rest. We see this in the ways environmental degradation has contributed to climate change, which in turn has negatively impacted our lives. The increase of floods and forest fires are examples. The same is true with people. When some people's work is devalued with low wages and poor working conditions, with scarce protections for their bodies, we harm one part of the web, which then affects us in ways that may appear roundabout but in fact are a direct result of our lack of attention to other's health and well-being. The spread of COVID-19 in meatpacking operations due to poor health guidelines is an example.

The intangible – beliefs, dreams, hope, memory, love, fear – is also bound to place. These are products of human thinking and humans are embedded in geographies. To be alive, to feel tenderness flood vein and artery, to make words in the company of fellow human beings, to reach for the starry sky, to be stirred by another, to marvel in high summer at a hop field, to step with your family into a mighty river, that is how we come to love a place.

The months of 2020 run together, so I'm not sure when I began reading *Braiding Sweetgrass*, by Robin Wall Kimmerer. I was going through boxes in my attic in August, and the book was recommended to me, but these events exist in a fluid merging of time, mixed with the sense of being trapped by the pandemic and making the best of it.

Inside my mother's blanket chest is a folded pink shirt, a birthday crown of dried flowers made by friends at Findhorn, a book by William Penn, and a braid of sweetgrass. The blanket chest sits under the eaves next to her boxes, most of which are filled with books. There are also carousels of slides of her garden and a portfolio of her paintings. When she moved west at sixty-one, she brought a library of books on horticulture, trees and Quaker and Pennsylvania history. Also, books by Native American authors, including stories of the Muscogee Nation and a book, reprinted in 1972, titled *The Folk Medicine of the Delaware and Related Algonkian Indians,* listing botanical names, common names, and the Native people's use of each plant.

When I read *Braiding Sweetgrass: Indigenous Wisdom, Scientific Knowledge and the Teachings of Plants*, each chapter felt like a friend because Elizabeth – Betsy – my far-ranging mother studied horticulture, attuned with plants, and did her best as a white woman of Scottish ancestry to understand Indigenous knowledge. If they had met, Elizabeth Dill Humes and Robin Wall Kimmerer might have had good conversations as artists, mothers, scientists, and teachers. A common message reverberates in their distinctly different lives: observe carefully, listen, gather, plant, connect.

***

In *Braiding Sweetgrass*, Kimmerer wonders whether it's possible that the transplanted newcomers from the European continent did not fully take root on the native North American continent. Maybe they mentally kept one foot aboard their ships in case it didn't work out. Maybe, because their relationship with the land and waters was tenuous, the colonizers didn't honor these gifts. "Gratitude comes first, but it is not enough," Kimmerer says.

Kimmerer, an enrolled member of the Citizen Potawatomi Nation and a professor at SUNY, asks her students and readers to look at our assumptions about nature now:

> You hear people say that the best thing that people can do for nature is to stay away from it and let it be. There are places that's absolutely true and our people respected that. But we were also given the responsibility to care for land. What people forget is that that means participating – that the natural world relies on us to do good things…You have to contribute to the well-being of the world.

If I had known about Kimmerer's book before my mother died, I could have shared it with the woman who taught me all I know about plants. Elizabeth learned the Latin names as a girl while walking with her father, who learned from his grandfather. She absorbed the *Systema Naturae* by the Swedish botanist Linnaeus, a system that Kimmerer describes as "a scheme designed to show the ways in which all things are related."

Elizabeth remembered this scheme even after a brain aneurysm put her in a coma three weeks after she moved in with me.

It was the year that the Mariners won the playoffs, and I remember newspapers at the hospital entrance with the headline: MIRACLE IN SEATTLE. For a week, my sisters, brother and I had taken turns by her hospital bed, a blessing and a privilege I see now, watching her sleep with a stainless-steel halo and a respirator. We waited to see if she'd recover from brain surgery, and after seven days, her eyes opened. Doctors asked the standard questions to gauge a patient's orientation to time and place: "Where are you? What year is it? Who is the president?"

"You look tired," she said to the medical staff. "Would you like to lie down?" We asked our own-questions, wondering what she'd lost.

"Elizabeth. What's the Latin name for monkey-puzzle tree?"

"Araucaria," she answered. When she didn't remember a plant or tree name, she knew the purpose, in her own lexicon. After weeks in a seventh-floor rehab wing, where she could make no sense of the view of treetops lining city streets, she was suddenly released. As I pushed her wheelchair through the doors, I hoped being outside would awaken more meaningful connections with the world around her.

"Hello, Child's Friend," she said to the faces of the blue and yellow pansies on the path.

***

I knew what it was as soon as I pulled the faded manilla envelope out of the box. The letter began with "Dear Elizabeth, The Orange Dill." This was the name that Jack, a friend from New Jersey, wrote on her get-well cards. Dill was her maiden name. Orange, the color of her tabby cats?

Elizabeth was a member of the Religious Society of Friends, or Quakers, which was how she met Jack. In the 1990s she had joined a committee to review the relationship of Quakers with the Lenape. In 1683, the Quaker William Penn wrote *William Penn's Own Account of the Lenni Lenape or Delaware Indians,* including a description of Lenape daily life, the language he was learning, and excerpts from early treaties. What happened to the Lenape in the next two centuries? Some descendants did survive the broken treaties, forced removals, and genocidal acts. At the end of the twentieth century, some Quakers in the New Jersey region wanted to shine a light on these injustices. Elizabeth joined with others on a committee to find out more.

The committee's work led them to Jack, a member of the Muskogee (Creek) Nation, whose ancestors farmed corn, beans, and squash in what is now Georgia. My mother and Jack worked on several projects and found they shared an interest in artifacts that told a complex story. I wish I knew more. Inside one of her boxes, I found a yellow sticky note that reads, "Dear Elizabeth: Thank you for generously allowing us to reproduce this book and map. Jack."

I held up Jack's typed letter, dated January 1997. "Warmest wishes from us for a happy, healthy, meaningful year. As you contemplate this new year please consider sharing and applying your incredible herbs, productive gardening, and horticulture knowledge."

Jack listed tribal councils in the Pacific Northwest that we could connect with and spelled out how she could apply her knowledge: "Tribes have herb and horticulture lore you can help preserve. You can help design gardens and plant herbs to sell. You can introduce new friends by asking them to buy from their markets." The letter ended with, "It only takes one Tribe, or family, to say yes. They will never forget you, your knowledge or your friendship."

After twenty-two years, reading the letter brought a stab of regret. I didn't help her do what he had asked. I took on her care when I was thirty-five and did what I could, but this seemed out of reach.

***

How do we partner with plants, animals, and one another to bring back balance? What if Elizabeth and I had read Jack's letter every January and asked, What now? His request was a gift. He saw her as capable of collaboration in a revival of Native agriculture when so many saw her as broken. She couldn't keep track of time. She lost her wallet daily. But perfectionism is a poison to relationships. Imagination is rich soil. What we can see in our mind's eye, we can bring into being. We can connect through stories and humor, working side by side.

I set up a pea patch garden for my mother where she grew beans and sunflowers. She gathered seeds of white clover and borage and saved them in her pockets to cast into manicured gardens when no one was looking. Over two decades, neighbors came to her for advice about their patio tomatoes and she planted window boxes of sweet alyssum.

I wish I could ask Jack for permission to quote his letter, but he's gone now. I found his obituary while I was writing this. He died in January 2017, the same month as my mother.

The letter that Jack sent to Elizabeth was written in 1997. Almost twenty-five years later, it brings me hope to find the Nature Rights Council putting into action the kind of projects Jack envisioned. Ancestral Guard works with children to develop gardens, deliver produce, and assist families with native agriculture. It also brings me hope to read in *Braiding Sweetgrass* that a Mohawk farming community is rooted on the shores of the Mohawk River. Imagine working together, spreading seeds.

ABOUT THE CONTRIBUTORS

Tele Aadsen is a writer, commercial fisherman, fishmonger, and lapsed social worker. She lives ocean-summers as a thankful guest of Lingít Aaní, Southeast Alaska, aboard the *F/V Nerka* (with partner Joel & cat Halcyon the Destroyer) and land-winters in the Coast Salish territory of Bellingham, Washington. She self-markets their catch through Nerka Sea Frozen Salmon and performs annually with Oregon's FisherPoets Gathering.

Celeste Adame, Muckleshoot, has been published in the *Santa Fe Literary Review, As/Us: A Journal for Women of the World,* and numerous Institute of American Indian Arts anthologies. She holds a master of fine arts in poetry from the Institute of American Indian Arts in Santa Fe, NM. She is currently fine-tuning her thesis, *Lovers' Landscape,* in hopes of getting it published.

Kelli Russell Agodon's fourth collection of poems, *Dialogues with Rising Tides,* was published by Copper Canyon Press in 2021. She is the cofounder of Two Sylvias Press as well as the codirector of Poets on the Coast: A Weekend Retreat for Women. Agodon lives in a sleepy seaside town on traditional land of the Chimacum, Coast Salish, S'Klallam, and Suquamish people. She is an avid paddleboarder and hiker. You can write to her directly at kelli@agodon.com or visit her website: www.agodon.com.

Maryna Ajaja was born in 1950 in Los Angeles and has been writing poetry since 1978. She moved to Seattle in 1969 and has also lived in Port Townsend and LaConner, Washington. During the nineties, she lived in Moscow and St. Petersburg, Russia. Ajaja is a graduate of Evergreen State College in Olympia, Washington. She has commercially fished in the waters of the Salish Sea and in Bristol Bay, Alaska. Since 1997, she has worked for the Seattle International Film Festival (SIFF), and is a senior film programmer specializing in Eastern European, Russian, Central Asian, Baltic, and Balkan cinema. Ajaja lives in Seattle's Dunlap neighborhood on Coast Salish land.

Kathleen Alcalá is a recipient of the Western States Book Award, the Governor's Writers Award, the International Latino Book Award, and two Artist Trust Fellowships. She has been recognized by Con Tinta and is a recent Whitely Fellow and a previous Hugo House Writer in Residence. Her most recent book, *The Deepest Roots: Finding Food and Community on a Pacific Northwest Island,* explores our relationship with geography, food, history, and ethnicity. Her first novel, *Spirits of the Ordinary,* was republished by Raven Chronicles Press in 2021. Born in Compton, California, to Mexican parents, Kathleen lives on Bainbridge Island.

Former Washington State Poet Laureate **Elizabeth Austen** is the author of *Every Dress a Decision* (Blue Begonia Press), two chapbooks, and an audio CD. She lives, works, and bird-watches in West Seattle and acknowledges this is unceded land of the Duwamish Tribe, past and present. Poems from her collection-in-progress appeared recently in the *New England Review* and *Spirited Stone: Lessons from Kubota's Garden.* Elizabeth provided on-air poetry commentary and interviews for NPR affiliate KUOW for nearly twenty years.

Ronda Piszk Broatch is the author of *Lake of Fallen Constellations* (MoonPath Press). Ronda's current manuscript was a finalist with the Charles B. Wheeler Prize and Four Way Books Levis Prize. She is the recipient of an Artist Trust GAP Grant. Ronda's journal publications include *Blackbird, 2River, Sycamore Review, Missouri Review, Palette Poetry,* and public radio KUOW's *All Things Considered.* Ronda lives in Kingston, WA, home of Suquamish and Port Gamble S'Klallam Tribes.

Barbie Brooking and her seven brothers and sisters grew up skiing on the slopes of Mt. Hood and swimming in the Columbia River. She now lives beside the Salish Sea on ancestral lands of the Suquamish people, where she and her late husband raised two sons. Her favorite jobs have been teaching for the Port Gamble S'Klallam Tribe and being a ranger at Katmai National Park. Her poems reflect her love of family and the natural world. She has shared her poems through *ARS Poetica, Salish Magazine*, and at poetry readings in her community.

Wendy Call is coeditor of the craft anthology *Telling True Stories* (2007), author of the award-winning nonfiction book *No Word for Welcome* (2011), and translator of *In the Belly of Night and Other Poems* by Mexican and Binnizá poet Irma Pineda (forthcoming in 2021). She was a recent Fulbright Scholar in Bogotá, Colombia, in Muisca territory. She lives, writes, and edits books in Southeast Seattle, on unceded Duwamish land.

Claudia Castro Luna is an Academy of American Poets Poet Laureate fellow (2019), Washington State Poet Laureate (2018–2021), and Seattle's inaugural Civic Poet (2015–2018). She is the author of *One River, A Thousand Voices* (Chin Music Press); *Killing Marías* (Two Sylvias Press), a finalist for the Washington State Book Award 2018; and the chapbook *This City* (Floating Bridge Press). Born in El Salvador, she came to the United States in 1981 and now lives, writes, and teaches in Seattle on unceded Duwamish lands. She is currently working on a memoir about her experience escaping the civil war in El Salvador.

Born in Seattle on the land known as PKa'dz Eltue by the Indigenous peoples of the Duwamish and Coast Salish Tribes, **Jocelyn Curry** is a graphic artist whose professional work has included her own expressive artwork, hand lettering and calligraphy for a broad range of clientele, and illustration for a variety of industries. She occasionally teaches workshops in hand-drawn maps. Her own maps created for protected lands feature native animals and plant species residing on those lands. She currently lives in Shoreline, Washington, the ancestral home of the Suquamish, Stillaquamish, and Coast Salish peoples.

Samantha Della-DeVoney was born and raised by Melissa Peterson in Neah Bay, WA, on the Makah Reservation and currently resides in Port Angeles on Klallam/S'Klallam territory with her daughter and partner. Sam enjoys working at Peninsula College as the Cultural Programs Manager for the Longhouse and in Evergreen State College's Native Pathways Program. She does her best to teach through Indigenous pedagogical approaches, with her culture and healing at the forefront of her heart/mind. Sam has her AA degree from Peninsula College, her BA in Native American Studies from Evergreen State College and is currently in the Master of Public Administration-Tribal Governance graduate program.

Risa Denenberg lives in Sequim, Washington, and works as a nurse practitioner for the Jamestown S'Klallam Tribe. She is a cofounder and editor at Headmistress Press, publisher of lesbian/bi/trans poetry, and curates the Poetry Café, an online meeting place where poetry chapbooks are celebrated and reviewed. She has published seven collections of poetry, most recently, *slight faith* (MoonPath Press, 2018) and the chapbook, *Posthuman*, finalist for the Floating Bridge Press chapbook contest (2020).

Alice Derry is the author of five volumes of poetry, most recently *Hunger* (MoonPath, 2018), along with three chapbooks, including translations of poems by Rainer Rilke. She taught for thirty years at Peninsula College, where she curated the Foothills Poetry Series. Since retirement, she has been active in helping local tribal members access poetry and has taught a number of community workshops. She has begun a series of essays on native plants. Her new poetry manuscript is *Asking*. She lives and works along the Strait of Juan de Fuca, land of the Klallam. Her website is www.alicederry.com.

Barbara Drake's newest poetry collection is *The Road to Lilac Hill*, from Windfall Press. She also writes creative nonfiction, including two Oregon Book Award finalists *Morning Light* and *Peace at Heart*, from OSU Press. She grew up in Coos Bay, Oregon, and has a BA and an MFA from University of Oregon. Drake is currently working on a book featuring her father's twentieth-century aerial photography of the southern Oregon coast. Retired from Linfield College, Drake and her husband live on a small farm in Yamhill County, ancestral home of the Yamhelas, part of the Kalapuya family.

Marie Eaton lives on the edge of Bellingham Bay in the shadow of Mount Baker, the traditional lands of the Lummi and Nooksack peoples. She is the Community Champion for the Palliative Care Institute (PCI) at Western Washington University, partnering with other community agencies to transform and support our human responses to living and dying. She has taught memoir and songwriting at Fairhaven College, The Northwest Writers Weekend, and the Northwest Women's Music (and Arts) Celebration. The poem published here was written in a morning writing collective that began at the onset of the pandemic, a daily writing exercise that provided respite and comfort through challenging times.

Kathleen Flenniken lives in Seattle, WA, on the traditional lands of Coast Salish, Stillaguamish, Duwamish, and Suquamish people. She is the author of three poetry collections, *Famous, Plume,* and most recently *Post Romantic* (University of Washington Press, 2020). *Plume* won the Washington State Book Award and *Famous* won the Prairie Schooner Book Prize in Poetry and was named a Notable Book by the American Library Association. Flenniken's other awards include a Pushcart Prize and fellowships from the National Endowment for the Arts and Artist Trust. She served as Washington State Poet Laureate from 2012 to 2014.

Susan Leopold Freeman likes to live with her hands dirty, from gardening or painting or creating mosaics, or most often from working on a salmon-stream restoration project on Washington's Olympic Peninsula. The restoration project has been supported by the Port Gamble S'Klallam, Jamestown S'Klallam, Lower Elwha S'Klallam, and Skokomish tribes, whose ancestors cared for the stream for millennia, and is the subject of the book *Saving Tarboo Creek,* which Susan illustrated. On the rare occasions when her hands are clean, she plays and teaches piano.

Tess Gallagher, the author of eleven books of poetry, lives and writes in her hometown of Port Angeles, Washington, on traditional land of the S'Klallam and Coast Salish peoples, and in her cottage in Co. Sligo, Ireland. Her most recent collection, *Is, Is Not,* documents political and meditational crosscurrents in her Irish and American lives. Gallagher attends to the work of her late husband, Raymond Carver, and participated in *Birdman* and *Short Cuts,* films centered on his stories. Her collection *The Man from Kinvara: Selected Stories*, published in 2009, is the basis for film episodes under development.

Carmen Germain lives on the Olympic Peninsula, the traditional homeland of Indigenous people of distinct tribes, cultures, nations, living languages, and dialects gathered close to the Salish Sea. She is the author of a chapbook, *Living Room, Earth* (Pathwise Press), and the collections *These Things I Will Take with Me* (Cherry Grove) and *The Old Refusals* (MoonPath Press). Her poems, paintings, and drawings have been published in *Poet Lore, Caesura, Oyster River Pages,* and elsewhere.

Jessica Gigot is a poet, farmer, teacher, and musician. She has a small farm in Bow, WA, called Harmony Fields, located on the traditional lands of the Coast Salish people, that makes artisan sheep cheese and grows organic herbs. Her second book, *Feeding Hour*, was published November 2020 with Trail to Table Press, an imprint of Wandering Aengus Press. Her writing appears in several publications, including *Orion, Taproot, Gastronomica, The Hopper,* and *Poetry Northwest.*

Sierra Golden graduated with an MFA in poetry from North Carolina State University. As winner of the 2018 Dorothy Brunsman Poetry Prize, her debut collection *The Slow Art* was published by Bear Star Press. *The Slow Art* was also a finalist for the 2019 Washington State Book Award. Golden's poems appear in *Prairie Schooner, Permafrost, Ploughshares,* and other literary journals. She lives in the Methow Valley, the traditional lands of the Methow and Okanagan people.

Iris Graville writes personal essays, memoir, profiles, and the occasional poem and has been published in national and regional journals. She's also the publisher of the online *Shark Reef: A Literary Magazine.* Iris's third book, the memoir *Hiking Naked* (2017), received a Nautilus Book Award. In 2018, Iris was the first writer-in-residence for the Washington State Ferries, drafting essays as the vessel coursed among the San Juan Islands. She's at work on a collection of those writings, *Writer in a Life Vest: Essays from the Salish Sea,* to be published in 2021. A retired nurse and environmental and antiracism activist, Iris lives with her husband on traditional Coast Salish lands, now called Lopez Island, Washington. irisgraville.com.

Sally Green's latest collection of poems is *Full Immersion* (Expedition Press, 2014). Honors include a grant from Artist Trust and a Stanley W. Lindberg Editor's Award. She has taught letterpress printing at the Naropa Institute and at Colorado College and poetry workshops at various literary festivals. Since 1982, Green has made her home on remote Waldron Island, where she has served as copublisher of the award-winning Brooding Heron Press. According to island lore, Waldron was a summer fishing residence for members of the Lummi Nation, especially, who called it Schishuney, "Fishing Place with a Pole."

Jean Hallingstad was born and raised in Anacortes on Fidalgo Island in the traditional lands of the Xws7ámeshqen (Samish) people, the fourth generation to live in their house and to garden their garden plot. After teaching for twenty-eight years, she retired three years ago and bought a farm west of Port Angeles in the watershed of the Elwha. During the year of lockdowns, she and her husband and two daughters have begun the work of restoring thirty acres of wetlands and neglected hayfields. She believes in planting trees.

Jana Harris has taught creative writing at the University of Washington, the University of Wyoming, and at the Writer's Workshop in Seattle. She is editor and founder of *Switched-on Gutenberg.* Recent publications are *You Haven't Asked About My Wedding or What I Wore; Poems of Courtship on the American Frontier* (University of Alaska Press), and the memoir, *Horses Never Lie About Love* (Simon & Schuster). She lives with her husband on a farm in the Cascades near Sultan, Washington, on traditional lands of the Skykomish people.

Sharon Hashimoto lives in Tukwila, Washington, on traditional lands of the Duwamish people. Her first book, *The Crane Wife,* was cowinner of the 2003 Nicholas Roerich Poetry Prize and was reissued by Red Hen Press as a Story Line Press Legacy Title in April 2021. Her second poetry manuscript, *More American,* was chosen by Marilyn Nelson as winner of the 2021 Off the Grid Poetry Prize. Recent poems of hers have been published by *Barrow Street, Sextant Review,* and *Shenandoah,* while her stories have appeared in *Moss, North American Review,* and *Permafrost.* In her retirement, she is working on a novel set in 1968 Seattle.

Alicia Hokanson, now retired from a long career teaching English, lives in Seattle on traditional lands of the Coast Salish, and she summers on Waldron Island, which was a fishing and berry-gathering destination for Lummi, Samish, and Coast Salish peoples. Her first collection of poems, *Mapping the Distance*, was selected by Carolyn Kizer for the King County Arts Commission publication prize. Two chapbooks from Brooding Heron Press are *Insistent in the Skin* and *Phosphorous*. Her new collection, *Perishable World*, was released by Pleasure Boat Studio in spring 2021.

Anita Leigh Holladay, a licensed massage therapist for forty years years, has been showing her photographs since 2005 in solo and group exhibits. Most of her photos are of the natural world, while others show the beauty of age in created objects. She has also written poetry for decades and enjoys reading it publicly whenever possible. She raised a daughter who also loves photography, gardening, and dancing, and who was brought up in loving contact with several Native American and First Nations elders. Anita has lived since 1992 on Orcas Island in Washington's San Juan Islands, a traditional home of many groups of Northern Straits Salish people.

Marybeth Holleman is author of *The Heart of the Sound* and *Among Wolves* and coeditor of *Crosscurrents North*, among others. Her poetry collection, *tender gravity*, is forthcoming from Red Hen Press. Pushcart-Prize nominee and finalist for the Siskiyou Prize, she's published in venues including *Orion, Christian Science Monitor, Sierra, Literary Mama, ISLE/OUP, North American Review, AQR, zoomorphic, Minding Nature, The Guardian, The Future of Nature,* and on NPR. Raised in North Carolina's Smokies, Marybeth transplanted to Alaska's Chugach Mountains, traditional lands of the Dena'ina, after falling head over heels for Prince William Sound two years before the *Exxon Valdez* oil spill. marybethholleman.com

Kathryn Humes is a writer and photographer who lives in Bellingham, Washington, the traditional lands of Nuxwa'7aq (Nooksack), Lhaq'temish (Lummi), and Coast Salish people. She received an MFA in creative writing from the Rainier Writing Workshop at Pacific Lutheran University. Humes works in the field of education, coordinating services to increase access for kids who are differently abled but are always kids first. She has also worked as a firefighter, Metro bus driver, and sign-language interpreter. Her poems have appeared in anthologies, on buses, and at the Bellingham Public Library as part of the Sue C. Boynton Poetry awards. kathrynhumes.com.

Kathryn Hunt makes her home on the coast of the Salish Sea, the ancestral lands of the S'Klallam, Chimacum, Suquamish, and Coast Salish people. Her second collection of poems, Seed Wheel, will be published by Lost Horse Press in 2021. She's worked as a waitress, shipscaler, short-order cook, bookseller, food bank coordinator, filmmaker, and freelance writer. kathrynhunt.net

Zann Jacobrown is grateful to live near the South Salish Sea on unceded land of the Suquamish Nation. Her paintings appear in many publications, including a recent book for Oxford University Press, and in over a hundred private collections. Jacobrown shares her essays and poems regularly and was the editor and lead writer of the educators' resource book *The Ancient Art of Conflict Resolution,* working with a dream team of Northwest Coast Indigenous educators and historians. She also leads arts and meditation classes and retreats and works as a rabbinic teacher and social justice rabble rouser.

Sara Mall Johani has been a working artist since 1974. She is a sculptor, designer, photographer, graphic artist, jeweler, and community inter-connector. She was the originator and cofounder of Wild Olympic Salmon (1987), a nonprofit community organization with the theme of salmon as teacher. She and her husband Tom Jay (1943–2019), also a sculptor, live in Chimacum where they sculpt, cast bronze, and teach bronze casting in The Lateral Line Bronze Casting Studio. We honor the Chemakum People, the Watershed Ancestors of the Chimacum territory. For thousands of years, the Native people of the Northwest coast honored the salmon in legends, totems, and paintings; we've tried to return its spirit to the artists.

Georgia Johnson lives on a small farm in the Skagit Valley, on Coast Salish ancestral land, surrounded by saltwater, alfalfa, mixed forest and in the company of a fine husband, cat, and all the resident critters you might imagine. She has made her way in the world by cooking, teaching, meddling, and writing. There are two collections of poems with her name on them, *Finding Beet Seed*, a collaboration with artists Maggie Wilder and Clifford Burke in 2001, published by Desert Rose Press, San Jose, New Mexico, and *Just Past Dew Point*, published in 2017 by Flying Trout Press, Bellingham, Washington.

Jill McCabe Johnson is the author of the poetry collections *Revolutions We'd Hoped We'd Outgrown* and *Diary of the One Swelling Sea*. Honors include an Academy of American Poets prize, Paula Jones Gardiner Poetry Award from Floating Bridge Press, and support from the National Endowment for the Humanities, Artist Trust, and Hedgebrook. Jill is editor in chief of Wandering Aengus Press and teaches creative writing for Skagit Valley College. Recent works are published or forthcoming in *Slate, Waxwing, Shark Reef, Book XI,* and *Crab Creek Review*. Jill lives in the San Juan Islands on traditional Lahq'temish (Lummi) land.

Irene Keliher is a fiction writer, essayist, and 2018 NEA Literature Fellow. Her work has won the Tobias Wolff Fiction Award, the Potomac Review Fiction Prize, and others, and appeared in *Narrative, Salon, CALYX, The Millions, The Weeklings,* and elsewhere. A former writing teacher and opera librettist, she's now a content marketing manager, which is not a career she knew about when studying for her MFA at the University of Houston. Raised in Indianola, Washington, in the ancestral territory of the Suquamish people, she now lives in south Seattle on unceded Duwamish land with her wife, sons, and too many pets.

Shelley Kirk-Rudeen has self-published two volumes of poetry, and her work has been included in several Northwest poetry journals and anthologies. Her writing studio in Olympia, Washington, is a few miles from the site of the Steh-chass village, one of several ancestral villages gathered to form the present-day Squaxin Island Tribe. "Zumwalt Prairie," the poem included in this volume, was written on the ancestral lands of the Nez Perce tribe. Although she has retired from professional life, some of her work lives on in interpretive signage and environmental outreach programs at parks and natural areas.

Jenifer Browne Lawrence is the author of *Grayling* (Perugia Press) and *One Hundred Steps from Shore* (Blue Begonia Press). Awards include the Perugia Press Prize, the Orlando Poetry Prize, and the James Hearst Poetry Prize. Her work appears in *Bracken, Cincinnati Review, The Coachella Review, Los Angeles Review, Narrative, North American Review,* and elsewhere. Former editor at *Crab Creek Review*, Jenifer lives on the Kitsap Peninsula in Washington within the aboriginal territory of the suqʷabš "People of Clear Salt Water" (Suquamish People). Say hello on twitter @JeniferBrowne.

Skye Levari currently lives in Indianola, on Suquamish land, surrounded by forested trails leading down to the expansive beaches below. She is a recent graduate from Fairhaven College in Bellingham, Washington, where she studied psychology and social justice. Poetry has become an essential buoy during these tumultuous times as she seeks direction amidst a pandemic and the increasingly unsustainable and unjust systems we exist within. Skye finds meaning in community organizing, creative facilitation, and mentorship with youth, and is currently working as an outdoor educator on Bainbridge Island.

Anna Odessa Linzer writes poetry and fiction. Her novel *Ghost Dancing* received an American Book Award; three of her novels were published as a limited-edition trilogy, *Home Waters*, by Marquand Books, one adapted into a performance piece. Her poetry, short stories, and novel excerpts have appeared in anthologies, textbooks, and literary magazines in the US, Canada, and France. She is a long-distance, cold-water swimmer. Descended from the Lenape, whose ancestral lands are along Eastern shores, Anna lives on Dabob Bay, once home to villages of the Twana and a hunting and gathering place for other coastal people.

Priscilla Long (she/her) is author of six books, most recently *Holy Magic* (MoonPath Press). She gratefully resides on the traditional lands of the Duwamish people. She is a writer of poetry, creative nonfiction, science, history, and fiction and a long-time independent teacher of writing. Her book of connected creative nonfictions is *Fire and Stone: Where Do We Come From? What Are We? Where Are We Going?* (University of Georgia Press). Her first book of poems is *Crossing Over* (University of New Mexico Press). Learn more at priscillalong.com.

Nancy Lord is a former Alaska writer laureate and the author or editor of ten nonfiction and fiction books, including *Fishcamp, Green Alaska, Beluga Days,* and *pH: A Novel.* Her work has appeared widely in journals and anthologies, including *Best American Spiritual Writing.* She teaches science writing for Johns Hopkins University and contributes regular book reviews to the *Anchorage Daily News.* Among her favorite activities are bird and wildlife watching, berry picking, and beachcombing. She lives in Homer, Alaska, on traditional lands of the Dena'ina Athabaskan people.

Paula MacKay is a freelance writer, researcher, and field biologist who has studied carnivores with her husband for the past two decades – with a current focus on wolverines. Paula served as managing editor for *Noninvasive Survey Methods for Carnivores* and earned an MFA in creative writing from Pacific Lutheran University in 2015. She has done communications work for numerous conservation groups and passionately writes about wildlife for magazines and other publications. Paula lives among great trees and myriad wild beings on an island in Washington's Salish Sea, on the traditional lands of the Coast Salish and Suquamish people. paulamackay.com.

K'Ehleyr McNulty is a member of the Ohlone Costanoan Esselen Nation of Monterey Bay and Carmel Valley. She grew up in Beaver Dam, Arizona, a tiny town off Interstate 15 between the red rocks of Southern Utah and brilliant lights of Las Vegas. Throughout her undergrad at UC Santa Barbara, she was a student athlete, worked three jobs, and was lucky enough to find a family with her Native peers. Now living on the contemporary and traditional lands of the Elwha Klallam people, she is honored to work with the Hoh, Quileute, Makah, Elwha Klallam, and Jamestown S'Klallam Tribes.

Mary Morgan is a happily retired special education teacher who lives in the Olympic foothills on traditional lands of the nə xʷ sx̣ʼayə̓ m (S'Klallam) people. Mary enjoys hiking, learning about all things natural, spending time with family and dear friends, and occasionally, when inspired, writing poems. Buddhism is a framework for her spiritual life. The pandemic has been a time of cultivating gratitude for all blessings in her life and renewing her commitment to protecting democracy and working for racial and social justice.

Linda Okazaki is a native Washingtonian, having lived on the Olympic Peninsula since 1980. She spent decades in the eastern part of our state earning both BA and MFA degrees from Washington State University. Her work is held in collections with the Washington State Arts Collection, Microsoft Corporation, King County Portable Works, and Seattle Art Museum, besides numerous other private collections. She is represented at Smith & Vallee Gallery in Edison, Washington, and Northwind Arts, Port Townsend, Washington. She deeply appreciates the influence of the S'Klallam traditional stories held in the land she has lived upon since 1980. lindaokazaki.com

Sara Marie Ortiz (Pueblo of Acoma) is a graduate of the Institute of American Indian Arts and Antioch University Los Angeles' MFA program. She's studied law, Indigenous education, global self-determination in Indigenous communities, journalism, radio, theater, critical theory, and film, and has worked in Native arts, education, and culture advocacy for over sixteen years. She has been featured in the *Kenyon Review, Ploughshares*, the *Florida Review*, the *American Indian Graduate*, and *Indian Country Today Media Network* and has presented at tribal schools, tribal colleges, conferences, and universities. She lives in Burien, Washington, and is currently the Native Student Success Program Manager for Highline Public Schools.

Meredith Parker (Mer) is an enrolled member of the Makah Indian Tribe. She is actively involved in the Makah culture: singing and dancing traditional family and tribal songs that have been passed down through the oral tradition from many generations past; recording her family's history from her grandmother's stories and research; making traditional regalia for cultural purposes and incorporating the traditional Makah values into modern-day life. She also enjoys capturing her homeland in photographic images, poetry, and memoir. She lives on the Makah Indian Reservation in Neah Bay, WA, and has two sons, two beautiful granddaughters, and two handsome grandsons.

Sandra Jane Polzin earned a bachelor of science in nursing with an art minor from the University of Washington, Seattle in 1979. Since then, she's taken classes in watercolor, nature journaling, drawing, calligraphy, and mapmaking. A Washington State Arts Commission apprenticeship in 2004 introduced her to weaving and cedar bark harvesting with master Tsimshian weaver, Loa Ryan. Other influences are Emily Carr, Hilma af Klint, Susan Point, Marie Coryell-Martin, Barbara Earl Thomas, and Ruth Ozeki. In addition to her studio practice, she is inspired by beach rocks, ravens, ancestors, and writing poetry. She lives in Seattle on the traditional territory of the Coast Salish people.

Rena Priest is an enrolled member of the Lhaq'temish (Lummi) Nation. She has been appointed to serve as Washington State Poet Laureate for the term April 2021–2023. She is a 2020 Vadon Foundation Fellow and the recipient of an Allied Arts Foundation Professional Poets Award. Her debut collection, *Patriarchy Blues,* was published by MoonPath Press and received an American Book Award. Her second collection, *Sublime Subliminal*, is available from Floating Bridge Press. Individual poems are featured at Poets.org, *Poetry Northwest, A Dozen Nothing*, and elsewhere. Learn more at renapriest.com.

Kate Reavey lives in the Dungeness watershed on the usual and accustomed lands of the nə xʷ sx̌ʼayə m, the Jamestown S'Klallam, who not only steward these lands and waters but lead important work in social and environmental change and advocacy. She honors and recognizes the generosity of the tribe. In her role teaching at Peninsula College, she recognizes their collaboration with the Makah, Hoh, Quileute, Port Gamble S'Klallam, and Lower Elwha Klallam tribes to envision and build ʔ aʔ kʷ ustəŋáwtxʷ House of Learning, Peninsula College Longhouse.

Bethany Reid has four books of poems, including *Sparrow,* which won the 2012 Gell Poetry Prize. Her more recent books are *Body My House* (Goldfish Press, 2018) and the chapbook *The Thing with Feathers,* part of *Triple No. 10* published by Ravenna Press (2020). She lives near Mukilteo, Washington, on traditional lands of the Coast Salish, Stillaguamish, Snohomish, and Suquamish peoples. Read more at bethanyareid.com.

Tina Schumann is the Pushcart-nominated author of *Praising the Paradox* (Red Hen), *Requiem: A Patrimony of Fugues,* winner of the Diode Edition's contest, and *As If,* winner of the Stephen Dunn Poetry Prize. She is editor of the anthology *Two-Countries: U.S. Daughters and Sons of Immigrant Parents* (Red Hen). Her work has appeared widely since 1999, including in *Ascent, Cimarron Review, Michigan Quarterly Review, Nimrod, Poetry Daily, Rattle, Verse Daily* and on NPR's *The Writer's Almanac.* For forty years she has lived in the city of Seattle, specifically the ancestral land of the Duwamish, Suquamish, Stillaguamish, and Muckleshoot Tribes. tinaschumann.com

Carolyn Servid recently moved to Colorado's Western Slope (homeland of the Northern Ute Indians) after living in Sitka, Alaska, for thirty-seven years (homeland of the Tlingit Indians). During that time, she cofounded and directed The Island Institute, a nonprofit whose programs focused on the nexus of story, place, and community. She was honored for that work with an Alaska Governor's Humanities Award in 2001 and an honorary doctorate from the University of Alaska Southeast in 2008. Her books include a memoir, *Of Landscape and Longing,* and three anthologies. Her essays have also appeared in various collections and literary journals.

Lauren Silver resides in Washington State in the traditional territory of the Suquamish people, the People of the Clear Salt Water, on the Kitsap Peninsula in the little town of Indianola. Her home is a precious little nest of a one-room cabin – a cabin who's a young beauty, not an old lady. Her neighbors, a mix of native trees and shrubs, inhale and exhale close by, on a ridge above the salty Salish Sea in a region whose conversations often refer to some form of this one word: water. Find her essays and poetry on her two blogs: apileofsticks.wordpress.com and gracewithindementia.com.

Leah Simeon is a citizen of the Spokane Tribe of Indians. Each summer, her family camps along the Spokane River on the reservation. Besides attending her Tribe's annual powwow, this is one of her favorite activities throughout the year. Leah teaches at the Muckleshoot Tribal School in Auburn, WA.

Ana Maria Spagna is the author of several books, including *Uplake: Restless Essays of Coming and Going, Reclaimers*, stories of elder women reclaiming sacred land and water, and two essay collections, *Potluck* and *Now Go Home.* Her first chapbook of poetry, *At Mile Marker Six,* will appear from Finishing Line Press in 2021. When she leaves the North Country, she'll return to the North Cascades where she lives on the ancestral lands of the Chelan tribe of the Syilx Okanagan Nation.

Ann Spiers is the inaugural poet laureate of Vashon Island and steward of its Poetry Post. Her 2021 publications are *Rain Violent* (Empty Bowl), *Back Cut* (Black Heron), and chapbook *Harpoon* (Ravenna Press Triple Series). Her previous publications are *What Rain Does* (Egress Studio), *Bunker Trail* (Finishing Line), *Long Climb into Grace* (FootHills), *The Herodotus Poems* (Brooding Heron), and *Volcano Blue*, *Tide Turn* and *A Wild Taste* (May Day). Ann humbly acknowledges she resides on the traditional lands of the sHebabS (Schwa ba sh), Vashon Island's indigenous people. See annspiers.com

Penina Ava Taesali is a Samoan poet. Her first collection of poetry, *Sourcing Siapo*, was published by the University of Hawaii, Ala Press, 2016. Her chapbook *SUMMONS: Love Letters for the People*, was published by *Hawai'i Review* in April 2018. Ms. Taesali earned her MFA in writing from Mills College in 2012. She dedicates her poem to the Kalapuya People of the Willamette Valley. She lives in Salem, Oregon.

Arianne True (Choctaw, Chickasaw) is a queer poet and folk artist from Seattle. She teaches and mentors with Writers in the Schools (WITS), the Seattle Youth Poet Laureate program, and Hugo House. Arianne is a proud alum of Hedgebrook, Jack Straw, and the MFA program at the Institute of American Indian Arts. A current Hugo Fellow, Arianne is working on a manuscript of experimental poetry. She likes being around plants and bodies of water.

For fifty-two years, **Charlotte Warren** and her husband have made their home on the Olympic Peninsula on the ancestral lands of the Jamestown S'Klallam, Lower Elwha Klallam, Makah, and Quileute nations. Here, the diversity of cultures and place, rainforest, mountains, and inland sea, inform her writing and sustain her spirit: salmon, cedars, hummingbirds, huckleberries, swans fattened up in Nash's fields, heading north to nest in the tundra. She is the author of two poetry collections – *Dangerous Bodies* (SFA Press) and Washington Prize winner *Gandhi's Lap* (*Word Works*) – and a memoir, *Jumna: Sacred River*, (SFA Press). She received her MFA from Vermont College.

Carolyne Wright's latest book is *This Dream the World: New & Selected Poems* (Lost Horse Press, 2017). A native of Seattle (unrecognized Duwamish *dxʷdəwʔabš* traditional land) who has lived and taught all over the country, and on Fulbright and other fellowships in Chile, Brazil, India, and Bangladesh, Carolyne has sixteen earlier books and anthologies of poetry, essays, and translation. A contributing editor for the Pushcart Prizes, Carolyne returned to Brazil in 2018 on an Instituto Sacatar residency in Bahia. She has received NEA and 4Culture grants, and a 2020–2021 Fulbright Scholar Award will take her back to Bahia after Covid-19 travel restrictions are lifted.

As editor of *Seismic: Seattle, City of Literature*, **Kristen Millares Young** honors the Duwamish Tribe's traditional land and ongoing presence. From 2021 to 2023, Kristen will be a Humanities Washington Speakers Bureau presenter. Named a *Paris Review* staff pick, her novel *Subduction* was a finalist for Foreword INDIES Book of the Year Award and two International Latino Book Awards. Anthologized in *Alone Together, Latina Outsiders* and *Advanced Creative Nonfiction*, her essays appear in the *Washington Post, Literary Hub* and the *Guardian*. A former Hugo House Prose Writer-in-Residence, Kristen was the *New York Times* researcher for "Snow Fall," which won a Pulitzer.

ACKNOWLEDGMENTS

Kelli Russell Agodon: "In Praise of Oysters" previously appeared on NPR's Seattle affiliate KUOW's website.

Maryna Ajaja: "Chimacum Cows" and "Port Townsend" appeared in *In Deep*, Wild Ocean Press, 2020.

Risa Denenberg: The three poems included here are from the chapbook *Posthuman*, Floating Bridge Press, 2020.

Kathleen Flenniken: "Horse Latitudes" and "Seven Seas" appeared in *Post Romantic*, University of Washington Press, 2020.

Tess Gallagher: Excerpts from "Writing from the Edge: A Poet of Two Northwests" from *Is, Is Not*. Copyright © 2019 by Tess Gallagher. Reprinted with the permission of the Permissions Company, LLC on behalf of the author and Graywolf Press, Minneapolis, Minnesota, graywolfpress.org.

Sierra Golden: "Some Ghosts" appeared in *The Slow Art*, Bear Star Press, 2018.

Alicia Hokanson: "World without Us" appears in the collection *Perishable World*, Pleasure Boat Studio, 2021.

Marybeth Holleman: "Wet" and "Bear" were published in *The Heart of the Sound*, paperback re-release by Bison Books, 2011. Original hardcover by University of Utah Press, 2004.

Irene Keliher: A longer version of "Wild Blackberries" was published as "Wild Blackberries: Finding Food, Family & Home" in *The Weeklings* in 2015.

Shelley Kirk-Rudeen: "Zumwalt Prairie" first appeared in *Windfall: A Journal of Poetry of Place* (fall 2006) and was also published in *We Are Just Passing Through* (2020).

Jenifer Browne Lawrence: "Landscape with No Net Loss" first appeared in *WA129: Poets of Washington* (Sage Hill Press, 2017)

Paula MacKay: "A Droplet of Wild Hope from the Epicenter" was adapted from an essay originally published in *Rewilding Earth*, March 21, 2020.

Penina Ava Taesali: "The Word of the Day" appeared in *Take a Stand: Art Against Hate*, Raven Chronicles, 2020.

Carolyne Wright: "Triple Acrostic: Orcas" was previously published in *For Love of Orcas: An Anthology*, edited by Andrew Shattuck McBride and Jill McCabe Johnson, Wandering Aengus Press, 2019.

Kristen Millares Young: *Seismic: Seattle, City of Literature* was published by Seattle City of Literature in the fall of 2020. The full text of her introduction and the collection of essays she edited is available as a free download at www.seattlecityoflit.org/seismic-seattle-city-of-literature.

EDITOR'S ACKNOWLEDGMENTS

It's been a profound honor to work on this issue these past months, grounding and inspiring me as we envision a path forward. First, deep bows of gratitude to all the writers and artists who contributed poems, essays, and art, especially the Indigenous writers and artists for trusting me with their words, maps, and stories.

My gratitude to Washington State Poet Laureate Rena Priest for her wise and eloquent preface and for her lovely metaphor of gathering. Heartfelt thanks to artist Linda Okazaki, whose work I've long admired, for her powerful cover image painted specifically for this issue. And, of course, a round of bows to Michael Daley and Empty Bowl for the invitation to guest edit this volume. I'm honored to be part of this community of writers and am grateful for this opportunity to dig deeper into its mission of focusing on "the love and preservation of human communities in wild places."

I want to acknowledge Fishtrap and the North Cascades Institute, where I've been blessed to teach over the past decade, and to all the naturalists, fellow poets, writers, and staff—too many to name—whose conversations have informed my thinking and deepened my commitment to writing and teaching on behalf of the earth. During the past year, I've been especially inspired by the writing of Dr. Bathsheba Demuth, Joy Harjo, Dr. Elin Kelsey, Robin Wall Kimmerer, Sy Montgomery, Arundhati Roy, Lauret Savoy, and Suzanne Simard.

I'm grateful to Laughing Moon Farm on Orcas Island for offering time, a view of the sea through the trees, a big table where I could spread out and reflect on all the submissions, and walks through the forest and down to the beach when I needed a break.

Each time I open the refrigerator, I read on a magnet: "It takes a group to raise a writer." I'm blessed with several, among them the Blue River writers and my fellow alums from the Rainier Writing Workshop, whose good work inspires and sustains my own. I'm especially grateful to Kathryn Humes for being an affirming sounding board for ideas and reflections throughout this project and for keeping me going with her empathetic listening ear, wise counsel, and good humor.

And finally, I'm ever more grateful to my husband, John Pierce, who was integral to producing this issue, for his affection, patience, calm energy, unwavering support, and steady companionship during the last eighteen months at home. I'll always be grateful for this time-out-of-time together.